THE FREELANCE
INTROVERT

The Freelance Introvert
Work the way you want without changing who you are

Written by Tom Albrighton (abccopywriting.com)
Cover illustration and design by Andy Carolan (andycarolan.co.uk)
Editorial support by Liz Jones (ljed.co.uk)

ABC Business Communications Ltd
100, George Borrow Road
Norwich
NR4 7HU
United Kingdom

Email: info@abccopywriting.com
Web: www.abccopywriting.com

ISBN 978-1-8380545-3-3

THE FREELANCE INTROVERT

WORK THE WAY YOU WANT
WITHOUT CHANGING WHO YOU ARE

TOM ALBRIGHTON

Contents

| MAKING A **START**

Yes, you can be a successful freelance introvert. No, you
don't need a personality transplant, and it doesn't have to
be a trauma either. And it all starts here.

Are you an introvert?

Do any of these sound familiar?

- I'm happy in my own company most of the time.
- I have just a few really good friends, mostly from a
  while back, and that suits me fine.
- I really love my friends and family, but sometimes
  I just need to be alone.
- I'm happy to let others lead the conversation,
  so I tend to stay quiet in company.
- It takes me a while to get to know people.
  Trusting them takes even longer.
- I prefer one-on-one meetings. Two's company,
  three's a crowd.

- If I spend too long with people, I start to feel strung out and off balance. Then I start acting crabby and withdrawn. That's when I know I need to get away and spend some time on my own to recharge my batteries.

- If I don't get time alone, I can't process stuff. I need to talk things over with myself before I can work out what I really think. I don't like being pushed into a decision before I'm ready.

- Since I spend a lot of time reflecting on my own thoughts and feelings, I feel like I know myself pretty well. I'm rarely surprised by my own thoughts, feelings or actions.

- I like hobbies and activities that I can do on my own. I'm not big on clubs and teams.

- Sometimes, I want to support a good cause, but I'm put off by the communal aspect. I look for ways to help without getting involved, like making a donation.

- When I'm learning something, I like to practise on my own until I'm ready. If I'm working on a personal project, I like to get it finished before I show it to anyone else.

If some or all of these statements resonate with you, you're probably an introvert.

The word 'introvert' is from the Latin *intro*, meaning 'inside', and *vertere*, meaning 'to turn'. So an *introvert* is someone who tends to turn inwards, towards their own thoughts and feelings, rather than outwards, towards other people or external events.

Some psychologists say that introverts find external stimulation overwhelming. So they look for places and activities where they can retreat from overstimulation. A situation that's easy or enjoyable for one person can be way too much for an introvert.

Introversion and extroversion aren't binary types, but two ends of a sliding scale. You can be very introverted, very extroverted, or somewhere in between. You can also pass through different states or moods – feeling outgoing one day, hide-in-your-shell the next.

Some people are ambiverts, with a balance of introvert and extrovert traits in their personality. If you felt that only some of the statements above applied to you, or if you felt that they only applied to certain times or situations in your life, you could be an ambivert.

If you're not sure whether you're an introvert or not, you could take a test like the Myers-Briggs Type Indicator (MBTI) to find out. The MBTI is based on the idea that each of us has a preferred quality within four categories: introversion/extroversion, sensing/intuition, thinking/feeling and judging/perception. That leads to 16 personality types overall, including eight different introverted types. You might recognize yourself as one of these.

Being an introvert isn't quite the same as being shy. Shyness is about being tense and awkward in company, sometimes unbearably so – and even extroverts can feel that way sometimes. In contrast, introverts can deal with company if they have to. They just prefer not to, at least for a lot of the time.

If you're an introvert, you're in the minority. Research suggests that extroverts outnumber introverts three to one.[1] Maybe that's why introverts are so misunderstood, and are often seen as being different or even deficient in some way.

Extroverts, in particular, often find it very hard to relate to introverts. They see them as arrogant, cold or aloof, and can't understand why they don't enjoy company. After all, the more the merrier, right?

To sum up so far: as an introvert, you like to live a certain way. Your way doesn't always fit with how life is, or what other people expect. That's fine as long as you have choices. But things can change when it comes to work.

Introverts at work

Many of us think of work as something we don't like, or would prefer to avoid. But we still spend around a third of our lives working (3507 days on average, plus up to 14,053 hours commuting).[2] So work is a big part of our lives, whether we like it or not – for introverts as much as anyone.

---

[1] https://www.sciencedirect.com/science/article/pii/S1550830716000379

[2] https://www.independent.co.uk/life-style/british-people-work-days-lifetime-overtime-quit-job-survey-study-a8556146.html

Do any of these sound familiar?

- Mondays are bad enough without all the office small-talk. Everyone's like, 'How was your weekend?' All I want to do is get to my desk and lose myself in some work.

- Our office is so noisy. People just walk up and start talking to you. You can't get anything done.

- Big meetings and brainstorms are the worst. Everyone wanting to have their say. I usually just sit there quietly, waiting for it to end.

- The things I dread most are team-building exercises, away days and office parties. Being forced to work or socialize with people I just don't like.

- Team projects just aren't for me. I like to work on things on my own, and only show them to others when I'm ready.

- I really wish I could work at home. I'd get far more done. But my boss would never allow it.

If you recognize some of these, you already know: working the nine-to-five can be really tough on introverts.

First, there's the simple and obvious fact that an organization is a group of people. So unless you work alone out on the road, or are lucky enough to get your own office, you'll spend most of your working day in the company of other people.

However, that's only the beginning. On top of that, many modern trends make working life even more social than it needs to be.

Open-plan offices put you in the middle of a chattering beehive. Anyone can interrupt you, any time, and they almost certainly will. Even at your desk, you're constantly distracted by the noise and movement around you.

Then there's the modern obsession with teamwork. More and more managers believe that they'll get better results by putting people together than allowing them to work on their own. As you know from your own experience, that's not necessarily true. Yes, a team can bring diverse people together, and throw up new ideas. But it still forces them to work as a unit, in the same way, at the same speed. What helps one team member may hinder another – and since introverts are frequently in the minority, they tend to come off worst.

A team dedicated to a project might just about work. Maybe you'll only have to meet once a week. But what if you get sent on an away day to 'build team spirit'? For an introvert, that's pure torment.

Sometimes, workers have to manage their own feelings and expressions in order to carry out their jobs. Sociologists call this *emotional labour*. For example, servers in a restaurant are usually expected to be cheerful. If they bang the plates down on the table or insult the diners, they're not considered to be doing their job properly.

Many workplaces make demands that are easy for extroverts to deal with, but constitute emotional labour for introverts. If the firm lays on a Christmas party, you're expected to enjoy it. If a colleague starts chatting in the kitchen, it's rude to walk away. If your team holds a brainstorming session, you're supposed to make a contribution. This endless effort to take part and fit in saps your energy and erodes your morale, making you dislike a job that you might otherwise love.

Fight through all that, and you might eventually get to sit down and concentrate on your work. But escape is still impossible, thanks to technology. You'll still be plagued by the constant pings of emails, calls or messages. It's supposed to be more efficient – but it can feel like you never get five minutes to think.

The strange thing is, you probably still do a lot of your actual hands-on work on your own. Sure, you spend a lot of time *talking* about it. But when it comes down to actually *doing* it, you're usually alone.

- If you're a designer, you create your layout alone.

- If you're a salesperson, you meet clients alone.

- If you're a manager, you put together your plans and presentations alone.

- If you're a craftsperson, you create your handiwork alone.

- And if you're a writer, like me, you tap out your drafts alone.

In other words, there's a tension between *where* you work and *how* you work – that is, between the nature of your workplace and what you actually do there.

That tension is even more painful if you're an introvert. You really *want* to use your skills and make a difference. But because you like to work alone, your workplace is always against you. While you just want to lose yourself in your work, working life keeps pulling you out.

But what if there was a way to resolve that tension?

Freelancer envy

Before I went freelance, I worked in a publishing house, and then a design studio. Along the way, I worked with many different freelance editors, writers, designers and photographers. And for many years, I looked at their lives with a profound feeling of envy.

I was stuck in an office designed by someone else, which always seemed to be either too hot or too cold. They worked comfortably at home, with total control over their environment.

I wore a shirt and tie. They wore jeans and hoodies.

I was grateful for my four weeks' holiday and flexitime. They came and went as they pleased, finishing work at 3pm for a swim or jetting off to the ski slopes for weeks on end.

I was under my boss's thumb. They seemed to choose what they did, and who they worked for.

Basically, I got all the crap that comes with work, with few of the benefits. But they seemed to get all the benefits with none of the crap. No wonder I thought, 'If only I could work that way!'

Now, if these freelancers had been a completely different type of person from me, none of this would have mattered. If they were barnstorming, go-getting extroverts, talking loud and pushing hard, I would have understood. I can't have what they've got because I can't do what they do, or be how they are.

But they weren't like that. They were like me.

During meetings, they listened a lot, only speaking to ask questions or confirm the brief, and left once they had the information they needed to start work. However, they were more than just yea-sayers. They had plenty of ideas of their own to put forward, and they weren't afraid to raise objections. Indeed, that was why we worked with them in the first place: because they brought us a strong and independent perspective that we just couldn't obtain in-house.

And yet, although they added real value to our team, and were practically recognized as members of it, they still maintained their independence and control. They helped our firm but without becoming part of it.

Clearly, freelance life was good to them. They didn't look like they dreaded every working day. They had demanding deadlines to meet, yet still seemed pretty chilled. And despite their introversion, they seemed confident and content.

I'd been told that freelancing was terribly insecure. But for these guys, it was all gravy. Business just seemed to flow to them, as if by magic; some were even supporting a family. Meanwhile, even though I was in full-time employment, I was sharing an apartment with a friend and permanently overdrawn.

How had they *done* that? How had they made the journey from a life like mine to a life like theirs? And how did they make it work now?

Since I didn't know, I was destined to spend my life as a cog in the machine, grinding out the nine to five.

Or so I thought.

Yes, you can be a freelance introvert

It's easy to see why freelance life appeals to introverts.

You work alone most of the time. You have no teammates, no colleagues, no boss. You decide when and how you meet people – if you meet them at all. You could easily go days, if not weeks, without speaking to another human about work. Yippee!

In terms of the work itself, you choose which projects to take on. You decide when and how to work, so you can use your time to best effect. You decide which calls, emails and messages to respond to. You are the boss of you. And you set up your workplace the way you want it.

Sounds like heaven, right?

However, there's a flip side to the coin.

As a freelancer, you're running a one-person business. No-one else is going to give you direction, organize your schedule or set your priorities.

That means going out to hustle for work from people you don't even know. It means setting your own prices and chasing for payment. It means actively managing your time and the way you work with clients. And it means building a network that will give you the opportunities and support you need.

Doing all that is hard enough for anyone – but it's particularly difficult for introverts. So while freelancing can be great for introverts, it still takes work.

You'll need to find the right balance between doing the things that feel natural to you, and pushing yourself to do the things you find a little bit more challenging. You'll need to learn some new skills and ways of thinking. And you'll need to build up the confidence to make it through when times are rough.

In this book, I'll share what I've learned about making that happen.

Who I am and why you should listen to me

I'm a lifelong introvert. As a child, I preferred playing alone – most often, writing and illustrating my own stories. I had a few friends, but not many. I didn't like team sports or group activities and I still don't.

When I grew up, I drifted towards office jobs where I could work on my own. My first 'proper' job was at a publishing house, and I moved on to a small design studio. When I was made redundant, I saw my chance to go freelance – and 15 years later, I'm still here. Through my work as a freelance copywriter and editor,[3] I've been fortunate enough to enjoy a good standard of living and support my family throughout that time.

Despite my introversion, I partnered with another (more outgoing) freelance writer to set up a trade organization for copywriters.[4] Managing the membership and organizing events took me way outside my comfort zone. On the whole, I'm happy I did it – but I was even happier to hand the reins over to someone else, refocus on my freelance work and watch the community thrive as a member rather than its leader.

I'm still an introvert. In fact, the older I get, the more introverted I seem to become. I love solo activities like running, cycling, gardening, gaming and writing. I still have a handful of friends who I'm close to, and rarely make new ones. And although it's ridiculous, I get anxious before going to pretty much any meeting or social occasion – even when I'll only see old friends.

---

[3] Visit my website at https://www.abccopywriting.com or connect with me on LinkedIn at https://www.linkedin.com/in/abccopywriting/

[4] Find out more at https://www.procopywriters.co.uk

I feel vaguely guilty about all this, but what can I do? The heart wants what it wants.

So, to sum up – I've been an employee, I've been a freelancer myself and I've spoken to lots of other successful freelancers along the way. And I've done it all as a confirmed introvert.

And that's why I think my advice might be useful to you.

Introversion is a strength, not a weakness

Before we go any further, I want to make one thing very clear. It's an important lesson that I've learned, and one you need to learn too.

Yes, you like to be alone. But that doesn't make you a freak, a villain or a psychopath. There is nothing wrong with being an introvert, and you're not inferior just because you are one – whatever you might hear in TV, magazines or social media. Your introversion is not a disease you need to cure, a character flaw that you need to correct or a weakness to be overcome.

In fact, being an introvert can give you many strengths:

- You're independent and self-motivated, and don't need to draw energy from other people to achieve your goals.

- You have a clear-eyed understanding of the world, and don't take your perspective from those around you.

- You listen carefully to what people say, remember what you learn and act on it.

- You take time to make the right decision and prepare for what's to come. You rarely give in to wild impulses.

- You know who you are, what you want and how you want to live. You don't measure yourself by others' opinions.

- You are excellent at focusing on a task until it's done, without going off at tangents or giving in to distraction.

- You're loyal, reliable and trustworthy.

I'm sure you can already see how these talents will help you freelance. Bring them together and you get a thoughtful, effective partner – someone clients know they can depend on. And in a world where too many freelancers are flaky and inconsistent, that's gold.

So you won't succeed *despite* your introversion, but *because of it*. You'll take the strengths you already have and turn them to your advantage. And you'll find ways to build up the areas where you need to improve until you're the complete article.

Introverts win too

When we think of a 'winner', we tend to picture an extrovert.

For example, think about the heroes and heroines you've seen in Hollywood films. How many were quiet, withdrawn and thoughtful? And how many were loud, outgoing and action-oriented?

The popular idea of a winner is a go-getter who achieves things 'out there' by getting involved, controlling situations and beating competitors. Or, if they don't achieve alone, they're vital members of a winning team. So if you're not really interested in all that, it follows that you must be a loser. Right?

Wrong. Introverts win too. Just look at Albert Einstein, Emma Watson, Bill Gates, Frank Ocean, Christina Aguilera, Meryl Streep, Elon Musk or Warren Buffett, who've all achieved great things as introverts. [5]

If you start thinking that winning equals extroversion, you can easily start to resent extroverts themselves. Just look at them, with their big smiles, easy confidence and winning charm. They're grabbing all the opportunities that should be going to talented introverts!

It's true that extroverts probably are better suited to certain jobs. For instance, it takes a pretty resilient character to sell door to door, or deal with unhappy customers at a service desk. Those high-exposure contexts are the ones where extroverts tend to shine.

However, extroversion has its downsides too. Because extroverts thrive on social contact, they can find it hard to work alone for long periods. Since interaction feeds their energy, they can be easily distracted by needless

---

[5] For more on the strengths of introverts, read *Quiet: The Power of Introverts in a World That Can't Stop Talking* by Susan Cain, Penguin, 2013.

conversations, calls and meetings. That wastes their time, and other people's too.

In conversation, extroverts feel bound to speak, even if they have nothing to say – which is actually just as likely to hurt their reputation as help it. And because they find listening hard, they miss out on valuable information and insight.

The point is that extroverts aren't better or worse than you – just different. Indeed, there are many situations where you need their strengths, and vice versa.

I called this book *The Freelance Introvert* because being an introvert and succeeding at freelancing isn't an either/or. You can be an introvert, build a great freelance career and enjoy an abundant lifestyle, all at once. And you can do it without changing who you are. You can be – forgive me – a wintrovert.

Now, let's talk about how you make it happen.

Takeaways from this chapter

- If you like to work alone and prefer your own company, you're probably an introvert.

- Introversion isn't an disease, a character flaw or a weakness. It is a strength.

- Freelancing is ideal for introverts, but you'll need to understand your own strengths and weaknesses to make it work.

- Extroverts are not invincible. Introverts win too.

2 CHOOSING YOUR FUTURE

Taking the plunge into freelancing can be scary.
Make it easier on yourself by planning your journey
before you set off.

Decide what you want

If you're currently in a full-time role, you might define
freelancing in terms of what you want rid of –
meetings, workplace politics, colleagues, your boss.
Basically, all the things we saw in chapter 1 that make
working life tough for introverts.

However, freelancing is more than just an escape from
the crap. It's a positive choice to do something new.
And if you want to make the most of it, you need to
consciously choose the way you want to go.

This chapter is about deciding what you want from
your freelance life. We'll look at the skills you want to
offer, the clients you want to serve and the rewards you

want to gain. Then we'll bring it all together in a mission statement that you'll write down.

The writing part is important, because committing goals to paper is extremely powerful. Once you've put an aim down in black and white, you're far more likely to make it happen. That may sound fanciful, but believe me, it's true.

As you work through this chapter, notice your thoughts. In particular, consider how you might be scaling back your ambitions because of what you think or feel about your introverted character. For the moment, just let yourself think big, without worrying about how it will happen.

Know your skills

Freelancing is about selling your skills. So the first step is to think about how your existing workplace abilities could combine to form your new freelance role.

To do that, go back through all the jobs you've ever held, and write down all the responsibilities you've had. For now, just focus on what you've done. Don't rule anything out because you think it won't interest clients.

Next, think about your life outside work. What talents do you have? What have you learned to do through hobbies or interests? Again, think big and broad.

Make sure you include 'meta' skills – in other words, skills that support other skills. For example, if you learned Spanish on Duolingo, you didn't just learn a language; you also learned how to manage your time and stick with a task over the long term. And you could turn those abilities to many other tasks.

As an introvert, you don't like blowing your own trumpet, which can make you reticent about your skills and strengths. So remember, this is a private exercise. Nothing you write down needs to see the light of day – either now, or at any time in the future.

Beyond job descriptions

If you've been in a salaried role, you've got used to fitting your skills to your job – squishing your ability into a box designed by your employer.

If you stay inside that box, you might start offering clients a service similar to your old job, or give yourself a label similar to your old job title. (Freelancing for your former employer might push you in the same direction.)

However, you can break out of the box. Your skills might be more widely useful than you thought. Plus, now you're freelance, there are no limits on how you develop them, expand them or recombine them to start offering something completely new. This is called 'skills translation' – you take a skill that was useful in a certain place, a certain time or a certain way, and reimagine it for a new situation.

As a first step, work through the points on your job description and turn them into generic skills.

For example, if one of your tasks was writing press releases, you could describe that as 'creating marketing content'. If you sometimes led team meetings, you could call that 'presenting to a group'. And so on.

Your qualities

Finally, consider what your skills say about your personal qualities. Have you shown creativity, initiative, lateral thinking, determination? Have you resolved a tricky situation or shown grace under pressure? Write it all down.

If you're not sure about your qualities, talk to people who know you well, and ask them what positive traits they see in you. As an introvert, you're naturally modest, so you tend to play down compliments, or even ignore them altogether. So make sure you really listen to what people say and take it on board – even if you think they're just being nice, or if you can't quite see what they're getting at.

When thinking about your qualities, express your introverted side in positive terms. For example, in the workplace, qualities like 'unassertive', 'quiet' and 'loner' aren't usually seen as strengths. So instead, use words like 'focused', 'reflective', 'hard-working', 'self-reliant' and so on.

Build your freelance work

Now, write all your skills and qualities on pieces of paper and start shuffling them around. How could they come together in new ways?

For example, let's say you have skills in graphic design and planning projects, plus the ability to learn independently and a strong interest in gadgets and technology. They could come together to form a new skill in web design or product design.

Or maybe you work as an event planner, but your real love is cooking. You could combine your understanding of both areas to offer a popup catering service for events.

Take time to reflect on everything you *could* do, without homing in on what you *should*. Some of your ideas might seem like fantasy, while others might be incompatible with each other. That's fine. You'll add in a dose of realism at the next stage.

Remember, your freelancing doesn't have to form a single 'job'. It could comprise two or more different roles in a portfolio career. The roles could be related, or they could be completely different. Maybe you'll spend half your time fixing computers, and the other half teaching clarinet. The strength of this approach is that you don't put all your eggs in one basket; the risk is that you spread yourself too thin.

You might also want to think about services that you've used, and found wanting. Could you do it better? Or there may be service combinations that seem to make sense, but aren't widely available. Could you combine two or more services in a way that helps clients? (Bear in mind that you could get others involved too, as we'll see in chapter 3.)

Finally, there's also the possibility of sharing what you've learned. For example, if you're a keen cyclist, maybe you could help others to build up their confidence on the road. Yes, it's a people-facing role – but maybe one-on-one for short periods could be OK.

Don't let your introversion hold back your thoughts. For example, don't think something like, 'I'd love to do more selling, but I'm just too shy to pick up the phone.' For now, just think, 'I'd love to do more selling,' and leave the limitations for later. There may be a way around them that you can't see until you start.

At the end of this process, you'll have written down a description of the freelance work you'd really like to do, and that suits the skills you have.

How will you help?

There are a number of ways people could use your service.

- At the simplest level is **delegation**. People are currently doing a task themselves, but they'd prefer not to. All you have to do is persuade them to let you do it instead. Your clients might fall into this category if you offer a service like gardening or domestic cleaning.

- The next level up is **expert help**. People know they can't do the job themselves (or, at least, not very well), so they turn to an expert. This covers my own clients, who ask me to write their marketing materials better than they can themselves, or improve the language in their academic articles.

- Then there are **problems in search of solutions**. Even though these people do need help, they may not know that it's available, or where to look for it. So you may have to work a little harder to bring them round to the idea of using you. For example, couples getting married may not know that there are freelance event planners who could manage their wedding for them.

- Finally, there are **learners**, who need your knowledge so they can do a task for themselves. Practically any skill can be taught to others, and there are many ways to teach it – one on one, in small groups, online or through the written word. Many freelancers find it more rewarding to teach their skills than actually use them.

Sometimes, these channels can be combined. For example, if you're a social media consultant helping a small firm with their online presence, you might take on some stuff they're currently doing, offer expert advice *and* share ideas for them to put into practice themselves.

Who will you do it for?

Knowing what you want to do is great. But to turn it into a freelance career, you're going to need clients. So the next step is to think about who might want your services, and be willing to pay for them.

Based on your experience, you might want to specialize in serving a certain type of client. For example, you might want to offer management consultancy to clients in the financial sector, or interior design for owners of period homes.

Location is important for some client types, but less so for others. As a copywriter, I can serve clients pretty much anywhere in the world, as long as they speak English. But if I was a painter and decorator, I'd probably want to restrict myself to clients within 50 miles or so.

Bring your thinking together into a simple client profile. For example, an IT consultant might define their ideal clients as 'SMEs within 50 miles of central London with 20 to 50 workstations'.

You might be thinking this is a bit pointless, since clients will be choosing you, rather than the other way around. Also, as an introvert, you might feel more comfortable just letting the market shape your freelance business, rather than trying to impose your will on it. But while the buying decision is for the client to make, you have choices too.

For example, it helps to decide which new-business prospects are worth pursuing, or which clients are worth going the extra mile for, so you can direct your efforts where they'll bring most benefit. And no matter what the situation, it's always good to stay in touch with your own *preference*, even if you ultimately decide not to act on it.

Thinking proactively about clients is also a valuable reminder that you always have a choice about who you're going to work for. We'll come back to this in chapter 5.

How much will you earn?

Wait, what? I can choose how much money I earn as a freelancer?

Yes, you can – and it's one of the most important choices you'll make.

In a salaried role, your earn whatever your employer is willing to pay. Sure, you can ask for a raise – but you only get one if they agree.

Freelancing is completely different. To some extent, your earnings are based on your skills and experience. But they're also based on how clients *perceive* those things, which is strongly influenced by your own personality and approach.

What's more, nothing is ever settled or set in stone. You have to hustle for every penny, close every deal yourself. Nobody is going to offer you more than you ask for, and you rarely have guarantees about the future. That can be worrying – but it's also liberating.

We'll come back to pricing in chapter 7. For now, just set an ambitious target for what you'd like to earn. 'Ambitious' means out of reach, but not out of sight. If you're not sure whether you can achieve your target, and it gives you a little flutter of excitement just thinking about earning that much, that's probably the right sort of level.

If you're coming off a salaried role, don't base your target on your salary. That's just climbing back into the box your employer made for you. There's no reason why your freelance earnings should reflect what you used to earn before.

Also, remember that being a freelancer means becoming a mini-business. You'll need to cover equipment, insurance, accounting support and possibly premises out of your earnings – and you won't be paid for illness or holidays either. So your earnings are really turnover rather than salary. The nearest thing you'll have to a salary is your profit, which is whatever you have left once you've covered all your costs.

What else will you do?

Unlike a nine-to-five job, freelancing doesn't have to occupy a solid block of time in every weekday. One of its great attractions is that you can fit it around other things – family, friends, hobbies and so on. So you can bring these other parts of life into your freelance planning.

Planning ahead is worthwhile, or things might not pan out the way you hope. For example, if you work at home, you might end up laden with more household chores than you anticipated, while your hobbies are completely squeezed out. Or, if your plans are 'all business', you might simply find that you get what you wish for: all work and no play.

Model successful freelancers

In chapter 1, I described the envy I felt for introverts who'd built successful freelance careers.

Later on, when I went freelance myself, I used those freelancers as a kind of template. They embodied how I wanted to run my working life, and my aspirations in terms of lifestyle, money and leisure. Basically, I wanted to be like them.

In neuro-linguistic programming (NLP), 'modelling' someone else's actions is recommended as a short cut to emulating their success. Instead of painstakingly learning everything they do, or have done, you simply set out to model their behaviour as best you can. As you do, your unconscious mind automatically absorbs the learning you need.

The great thing about modelling yourself on others is that it gives some concrete, visual detail to your freelance future, so it's not a complete leap into the unknown. Instead of writing your story on a blank page, you borrow details from someone else's story to help you make a start.

Write your future

Having answered the big questions about your freelance life, bring the answers together into a written description of your future.

Just to recap, you've focused on:

- The skills you offer

- The clients you're going to serve

- How much you want to earn

- How life outside work will fit into the picture

- People you might want to emulate or model.

For example:

> *I have skills in event management and a lifelong love of cooking. Building on that, I'm going to make a living from my popup burger stand, catering at events and parties. My clients will be anyone in a 50-mile radius who's willing to pay my basic rate, which will be £500 per event. By the end of my first year, I want to be catering for two events a week, making around £50,000 and taking three weeks' holiday a year. Then I'll increase my rate and maybe bring in others to help, so I can do fewer events and spend more time with my kids.*

As I said earlier, writing things down has awesome power. So that's why it's important to actually write your future, not just think about it. You don't necessarily have to look at the writing again – just keep it safe.

Tell your story

An alternative way to write your future is as a story. You can start in the past, explain how you got where you are now and then continue the story on into your future.

Writing a story makes sense of your experience, by giving order to life's twists and turns. Your story can also illustrate the values that put the heart and soul into your work – the 'why' behind the 'what' of your freelance life.

Your story doesn't have to be a great work of literature. It just has to be true, clear and meaningful to you.

For example:

> *For as long as I can remember, I've loved cooking –*
> *especially for big groups and parties. After college,*
> *I wanted to train as a chef but it didn't work out*
> *and I ended up working in event management.*
> *Now, 10 years on, I'm ready to return to my first love.*
> *I help party organizers and event managers with an*
> *affordable popup stand selling delicious burgers.*
> *In future I'll be adding more dishes, occasions and*
> *team members.*

As you can see, stories are way more vivid and memorable than straightforward descriptions. A story will probably inspire you more, even if no-one else ever sees it. However, it also points the way forward, to how you, as an introvert, can make your skills face outward and communicate your value to the world – which we'll explore in chapter 6.

For example, your story could play a marketing role on your LinkedIn profile or 'About me' page. It could also help you answer when clients say, 'So, tell me a little about yourself.' If you tend to keep your cards close to your chest – as most introverts do – a little preparation will give you the confidence to reveal the things you want to.

The law of attraction

The law of attraction states that whatever you focus on becomes your reality. When you vividly imagine your future, you're more likely to bring it about.

Why am I sharing a quasi-mystical idea in a business book? Basically, because it works.

When I started out freelancing, I wrote down a vision of how I wanted the future to be. I wrote about both sides of my life: my workspace, my clients and my earnings, but also my friends, family life and leisure time.

Once I'd written my vision, I closed the document and pretty much forgot about it. But over the following years, slowly but surely, it *did* come true. Somehow, that vision took root in my unconscious and guided my choices, allowing me to attract the things I wanted in my life.

Here's how to make the law of attraction work for you:

- **Be specific**. Decide *exactly* what you want to happen, and describe it in rich sensory detail.

Imagine and write down what you'll see, hear, touch, taste and smell when your dream comes true. Find or create images of what you want – your office, your home, your travels, whatever. (I even made an image of my future bank statement.) Make your future as real as you possibly can.

- **Be absolute, not relative.** 'More clients' could mean one more client. 'More money' could just mean £1 more. 'More free time' could be one more hour. Decide how many and how much – for example, 10 more clients, £10,000 more earnings, 10 hours of free time per week.

- **Be ambitious, but realistic.** Your target should be 'out of reach, but not out of sight'. It should feel daring, but not daunting. You should feel unsure whether you can actually do it, but still excited by the thought that you could.

And here are some things to bear in mind:

- **You'll attract opportunities, not outcomes.** In other words, you'll still have to work to make your vision a reality. If you want cash, it won't arrive in a gift-wrapped box with a bow on top. Instead, you'll get the chance to earn it. If you want happy, loyal clients, you'll still have to close deals and deliver value.

- **Be careful what you wish for.** The law of attraction works for better or worse, and it doesn't care about consequences. I once set myself an earnings target that I wasn't sure I could reach. As it turned out, I could – but it was a pretty exhausting year, and at the end of it, I seriously questioned whether I wanted to set that target again.

- **Attraction works in mysterious ways**. Your vision may come true through unexpected events, or at unexpected times, or with unexpected people. You might even be tempted to call it luck or coincidence. Maybe so – but the point is that *chance favours the prepared mind*. The first step in taking an opportunity is being aware of it. By clearly describing your goal, you attune your mind to the future choices that will bring it about.

The great thing about the law of attraction is it keeps you focused on the destination. When you go freelance, it's easy to get stuck in an endless present, constantly reacting to clients or juggling work and home demands. From time to time, you need to remember what you're doing all that stuff *for*.

So, you've decided your vision. Now you just need to make it a reality. And we'll explore exactly that in the next few chapters.

Takeaways from this chapter

- Decide what you want from your freelance work, and where you want to end up. Don't set off without a destination.

- Look at *all* your skills and qualities, and determine how you can use them to help clients.

- Decide what work you want to do, who you'll do it for and how much you want to earn from it.

- Write down your desired future so it's more likely to come true.

- When setting targets, be concrete and absolute, not vague and relative.

3 *GETTING* **SET UP**

Prepare yourself for freelance life by thinking about where and how to work, who will support you and how you'll separate your work and life.

Your workspace

One of the first decisions you'll need to make is where you're going to work. The two main options are working at home and renting an office space or workshop somewhere else.

Working at home can seem very attractive to introverts, for several reasons.

First, you can arrange your workspace exactly as you want it. You can stay close to the books, music, films, pictures, garden, or pets that make you who you are, and draw strength from them whenever you want.

When you think about it, having a job means spending most of your life travelling away from your own space, into a domain that someone else controls. As a freelancer, you can stay on your home turf. That alone can make a huge difference to your mood, almost regardless of what happens with work.

Second, you can concentrate without people distracting or interrupting you. You can physically move around without fear of unwanted interaction; no-one will accost you while you make coffee or use the shredding machine, and hijack half an hour of your time. And if you don't feel you can face anyone at all, you don't have to.

The downside is you might become *too* introverted. Your tolerance for company might go down, or you might find that you find socializing more daunting than you did before. That's not such a big deal in itself, but it can be a problem if you need to go to a meeting or a conference, and it becomes a big obstacle in your mind. There might be times where a little face-to-face with the client would really help a project, but you shy away from it because you're so accustomed to working alone.

So you might want to do a little networking, meet another freelancer for coffee or just chat to other parents at the school gate to stop your 'interaction muscles' atrophying from lack of use. Events organized by professional associations can be a great way to get out and meet people with whom you have a lot in common – so you know you'll already have a good rapport, and the conversation will always flow easily.

So far, I've assumed that you can easily achieve solitude and seclusion at home. But if you share your space with others – particularly young children – that might not be the case. So you might want to consider renting somewhere else instead.

Having a workspace away from home can be a great way to put a little bit of interaction in your day. You might meet a friendly fellow freelancer, or even score a new client. However, you'll still want full control over where and when you see people. That will probably mean a door that you can close, and almost certainly not an open-plan office where you're laid open to other people's noise and chat.

Renting can feel like a big financial commitment, particularly when the alternative (working at home) is effectively free. So look for the most flexible arrangement you can – month-to-month, ideally, or failing that a shorter lease with a break.

To dispel your financial fears, get clear about costs and consequences. When I rented an office, I was anxious that I might dig myself into a financial hole that I could never climb out of. So I created some simple spreadsheets showing my projected cash flow for the duration of the lease – essentially, fees coming in minus rent going out, in two different scenarios.

In the first version, my monthly earnings stayed flat, and while I would indeed end up in some debt, it wasn't as much as I'd feared. In the second version, my earnings kept growing at the rate they had up to that point, and the rent became less and less significant over time. These two projections gave me the confidence to sign the lease – and in the end, reality surpassed both of them by far.

Your equipment

Just as an employer needs to provide the right tools for their workforce, so you need to give yourself the kit you need to work – a decent desk and chair, a computer that's powerful enough, and so on.

Buying this stuff can get costly, especially if you're getting all of it in one go. So remember that these are *investments* in your freelance business, not just expenses. You're building the vehicle that will take you where you need to go.

However, the right kit can also help psychologically. For example, buying a laptop allows you to work on the go, which can make a big difference to your productivity. But the ability to work where you want can also enhance your mood. Also, buying professional equipment gives you a sense that your freelance business is a real and solid enterprise that deserves investment – not just something that you're trying out to see how it goes.

However you set up your business, you'll need a way to keep track of your accounts. There are many options for this; I use an online platform called FreeAgent. One of its best features is automatic invoice chasing: once an invoice is overdue, the system sends regular reminders until it's paid. Before I had this, I used to put off chasing invoices because I didn't want to upset my clients. That kind of tact is way too expensive.

Another important bit of kit is a contract, or a set of terms and conditions. This sets out the legal basis for your freelance work for your clients, including aspects such as what you will and won't do, how disagreements will be resolved and who owns the intellectual property rights in the finished work. The great advantage is that if things do go wrong, you can simply point to the written agreement, rather than having to impose your will and say what you think should happen. It's not you, it's the contract.

Your physical health

A lot of freelance work is done with the mind. However, a freelancer is more than just a brain in a vat. Your mind and body are two halves of one system – and it's vital to keep *both* of them in good condition.

If you work at home, it's easy to neglect physical fitness. If you do, you'll soon find it starts to affect your mood, and that in turn will affect the quality of your work. Freelancing demands energy and stamina, so your physical health supports your success.

Choose an activity you enjoy and make time for it in your day. You're an introvert, so it will probably be something solo, like running or cycling. I personally find it most beneficial to exercise first thing in the morning. It gives a great feeling of balance and alertness, which then carries through into the rest of the day.

Sleep is vital for both physical and mental health, so make sure you get plenty. Not only will it prepare you for the day ahead, you'll find your unconscious mind solves problems while you sleep. It's often far more productive to leave a problem overnight than sweat it long into the evening.

Your mental health

When you work on your own, the most likely mental hazard is stress.

As an introvert, you're happy to work alone for long periods. In fact, you find comfort in becoming completely absorbed in your work. But the flip side is that you may go *too* deep into your work, to the point where you start to lose perspective.

Problems that you can easily overcome get blown out of proportion. You start second-guessing clients' intentions, or reading too much into things they've said or done. You become more and more overwrought, and because you're an introvert, you tend to sit with the problem alone, instead of reaching out for help.

Therefore, the simplest way to regain perspective is to actually speak to the client. Often, that phone call you've been dreading for days turns out to be far easier, and far more helpful, than you imagined. It might even be that the client has been turning over related concerns in their own mind, and the call is a huge relief for both of you.

Apart from that, it's always positive to get yourself some space. Don't just sit there, stewing in your own juice. Step away from your computer; put down your device. Go out for a walk, ideally in a natural environment. If you can't do that, just move to a different room. Listen to music or watch some TV, just to get your brain into a different place.

Another good antidote for stress is to reflect on your own past experience. Whenever I start stressing about my workload, my partner often points out that things have always worked out in the past. Of course, they didn't just 'work out' on their own – I busted my ass to meet those deadlines. But basically, she's right. I've come through this kind of situation before, and I can do it again.

You can do something similar when you're feeling unsure of your own ability. Think back to a time when you took on a new challenge, and learned how to overcome it – maybe at work, maybe somewhere else. The lesson from that memory is that while you might not know what to do right now, you know how to find out. You have gone from not knowing to knowing before, and you can make that journey again. (There's more on this in chapter 8.)

Problems feel even worse when you're under time pressure. We'll look at managing your time in the next chapter.

Finally, if you feel that your mental problems are getting too much for you, seek expert help.

Feeling hassled about work is one thing; full-blown anxiety or depression is quite another. If you think your negative feelings are something more significant than simple work stress, speak to a doctor or counsellor.

Your network

You may like to work alone, but you still don't have to be lonely.

Even introverts need a helping hand from time to time, which is why you need a network of friends and contacts who can offer you support and encouragement along the way.

Friends and family are the most obvious candidates. However, they may not be able to relate to every detail of your new freelance life. Specifically, people with regular jobs can't always understand what it's like to have an uncertain income, or to sort out your own admin as well as the hands-on side. So be thankful for their support, but don't expect them to appreciate all the ins and outs of running a freelance business.

If you're coming to freelancing from an in-house role, your former colleagues could be a great source of support (and maybe work). They know very well what you're capable of, so chatting to them can boost your confidence in the value you offer. However, when you meet up, you might find they're still moaning about the same old office politics – so give yourself a pat on the back for jumping ship. (They'll probably be trying to hide their own envy.)

Other freelancers can be a great source of support. Even people who are technically your competitors can turn out to be far more friendly and open than you might expect. Hit them up for general advice, valuable discussions about pricing or a good old moan about clients from hell. Don't confine yourself to people who do the exact same work as you – you can pick up useful tips and perspectives from freelancers in other areas too.

Social media can be a great way to get support on tap, without the hassle or time commitment of meeting in person. Use Twitter to follow freelancers and experts in your area, or search Facebook for groups you can join. LinkedIn is a great place to talk about work and freelancing – just ask a question and watch the replies roll in.

Finally, there are organizations devoted to particular jobs or skills that you can join. They're often a great source of information, particularly on tricky topics like financial or legal matters. Search online or ask on social media and you'll soon find one that suits.

Your collaborators

In 2011, I founded the Professional Copywriters' Network (now ProCopywriters) with Ben Locker.[6]

Ben was also a copywriter. However, while we both did similar work, our characters could hardly have been more different.

While I was a details person, Ben was all about the big picture. While he was setting ambitious targets, I was worrying about how we'd make it all happen. His politics were conservative, while mine are more progressive. He'd worked as a classroom teacher, while I'd spent my life in offices. And, last but not least, while Ben had the easy charm and loquacity of someone who is naturally confident and outgoing, I was a classic introvert.

However, none of that stopped us from making a success of our venture. Over the next few years, we grew the organization to have hundreds of members, a thriving website and a popular annual conference. And we did it not *despite* our differences, but *because of* them. We had complementary strengths, so both of us could make our unique contribution while compensating for the shortcomings of the other. And that allowed us to achieve something together that neither of us could have managed on our own.

We saw in chapter 1 how teamwork isn't always kind to introverts. However, there's a big difference between

---

[6] Find out more at https://www.procopywriters.co.uk

being thrust into someone else's team and willingly creating one of your own. There's also the question of scale: while a team that includes a dozen people will probably be far too hectic for an introvert, a more low-key affair with just one or two other members might be something you can tolerate, or (whisper it) actually quite enjoy.

The great thing about collaboration is the chance to choose your own colleagues. While workplace co-workers are imposed on you by management, you have completely free rein over which freelance partners you decide to work with. So you can choose someone who not only compensates for your introversion, but respects it too. Someone who's happy being an extrovert, but appreciates that talking loud doesn't necessarily mean you have all the answers.

There are many ways to collaborate with others. You might partner up with a fellow freelance on a project-by-project basis, working together to meet particular client demands. Or you could create something longer-lasting – a banner under which you can market your combined skills. It doesn't have to be something as expensive or committed as a co-founded company; it could be just a brand or a website that you use to promote your joint offer.

Collaborators can also be an important source of support. They might give you a new perspective, or valuable feedback, that you just can't achieve on your own. Or they might offer validation and encouragement when your confidence is low. Even introverts need someone to talk to from time to time.

Whatever collaboration you choose, it has to add value for you. Be sure that you are getting a fair share of the rewards, in return for a fair share of the effort. The key to this is communication – making sure that you and your partner are always on the same page. Sometimes, partnerships are attractive and lucrative for a while, then fade as the participants naturally drift apart. So if that happens, let it.

Your suppliers

The clichéd view of a freelancer is the 'chief cook and bottle-washer' who does everything from making coffee to preparing accounts. But while freelancing obviously means going solo, that *doesn't* mean you have to do everything yourself. Instead, you can use outsourcing to get outside support with business tasks.

When you outsource, you trade money for time. By paying someone else to do something, you buy back the time you would otherwise have to spend on it. Then you use that time to do something more valuable. The result is that your business moves ahead on multiple fronts, instead of being just you plodding along on your own.

The outsourced task might be something that someone else can do better, like preparing your accounts or drawing up a contract. Unless you really want to put in the hours learning accountancy or law, it makes more sense to use a professional. The ideal setup is one where you can call on their expertise whenever you need it – not just at set times, like preparing your tax return.

Or you might just want to outsource a task that you *can* do, but still prefer to delegate. For example, I often use telephone interviews to gather information for writing jobs. Instead of spending an hour or two transcribing the audio recordings myself, I send them off to a specialist company.

For introverts, modern methods of outsourcing can offer a great balance between productivity, collaboration and solitude. Once you've outsourced a task, it's great to feel that someone is beavering away on it on your behalf, while you work on something else. However, you are in fact still alone, sitting in your workspace, with your equilibrium and concentration intact. It's like teamwork, but without the team.

The financial maths of outsourcing is pretty simple. If the cost is small in relation to your own fee, and there isn't too much hassle involved for you, it's worth doing. Sometimes, you might want to outsource even if you don't make that much on the deal, just so you can hang on to a client – but don't let this become the norm, or you'll end up spinning loads of plates for no reward.

The more challenging the work, the trickier it is to outsource it. Many freelancers (myself included) have dreamed of a setup where they farm all the work out to other freelancers, take a cut off the top and spend all day on the beach. The problem is finding reliable partners who are willing to work this way at a price that works, and whose work you are happy to pass straight on to clients without checking every detail. And the better the supplier, the bigger your risk of getting cut out of the loop.

Basically, if you go down this route, you are well on the road to becoming an agency or a small firm, with all that entails. So consider carefully if that's really what you want – particularly as an introvert – or if you actually prefer the flexibility and control of remaining a sole agent.

Setting boundaries

A regular job has very clear boundaries. You work in a particular place (like an office) at particular times (like nine to five). Outside that place, and those times, you're officially Not Working, so it's easier to switch off – in theory, at least.

One of the hazards of freelancing is that your work seeps out into the rest of your life. If you're not careful, you start working, or just thinking about work, more than you should. Then you get stressed and over-tired, and that leads to substandard work. You might even wind up being turned off freelancing altogether.

To stop all that before it starts, you need to establish firm boundaries that will keep your work safely inside its box.

There are three types of boundary to consider: physical boundaries (around places), temporal boundaries (around times) and psychological boundaries (around your thoughts).

Physical boundaries are about having a designated place where you work most or all of the time. If you work at home, the best place is probably far away from the busy heart of the home, which is often the kitchen. Out of sight is out of mind, so have a door that you can close when you're not working. Otherwise, just catching sight of your desk on the way to the bathroom may evoke unwelcome thoughts of work, or even draw you back into 'just finishing something off'.

Temporal or time boundaries are about having set times to work. Obviously, part of the appeal of freelancing is the chance to work when you want. But it's still worth having some sense of what your hours are, so you know when to start and stop work. Decide when you'll start, how long you'll take for lunch and when you'll knock off for the day. Switching to a non-work task, like preparing dinner or taking exercise, is a good way to impose a hard stop at the end of the day.

Be realistic about how much you can do in a day. It's nine to five for a reason – longer hours often bring diminishing returns. You can easily end up slumped at your desk at 8pm, supposedly 'working' but actually zoned out and producing nothing of value, because your aching brain simply won't do any more. Believe me, you will finish that job a *lot* quicker if you knock off now, get a good night's sleep and aim for an early start in the morning.

By the same token, watch out for weekend working. I'm sure every freelancer has done it, whether through a scheduling screw-up, a client's actions or just for the money. But I find that whatever time I borrow from the weekend, I have to pay back the following week – with interest. Your mind needs time to recuperate, and it will sorely resent you forcing it to work overtime. If a weekend stint is genuinely unavoidable, do a specific, bounded task within a specific time-slot – then pack up, forget work and go have fun.

The last type of boundary, and the hardest to enforce, is psychological. Basically it means that, as far as possible, you don't think about work unless you're actually working. As we've seen, introverts have a strong tendency to 'turn inwards' and sit with their problems until they're solved. So imposing this sort of boundary might be more difficult for you.

The other two types of boundary support psychological boundaries. If you can't see your desk, you're less likely to think about work. If you stop work on time each day, you have time to mentally 'come home from work' before the evening starts.

Beyond that, though, this is a boundary that you must build in your head, by making conscious decisions not to think about work at the wrong time. When you notice thoughts of work arising, acknowledge them, then gently 'put them down' and choose to think about something else.

If you like a drink, it's tempting to try and annihilate your work thoughts with alcohol. That's the idea of the Friday night after-work drink – a few beers, a cathartic moan and then you're ready for the weekend. Actually, I now find that alcohol just shakes up my thoughts and feelings in a disorienting, fairly unpleasant way, leaving me feeling worse than before. So I try to use it more as a reward for success than a 'fix' for problems.

Takeaways from this chapter

- Invest in the right workspace and equipment from the start.

- Take care of your physical and mental health, or your work will suffer.

- Even as an introvert, you still need a network to support you.

- You don't have to do everything. Outsourcing can save time and boost your earning power, without impinging on your introvert working style.

- Maintain boundaries around your work, so it doesn't take over your life. Don't let introversion curdle into brooding.

4 MANAGING YOUR TIME

Time is your most precious resource. Use it wisely.

It's about time

As a freelancer, your most precious resource is time. It's the one thing you have to sell, and you only get paid for the time you work. So in this very basic sense, time is money.

However, time is more than that. You're not just a robot that operates from nine to five. To move towards your bigger goals, you'll need to consciously decide to spend your time on other things, like developing your skills. And you'll need to take some time to reward yourself, and to take care of yourself too.

Going freelance gives you control of your time. The only schedules and deadlines are the ones that you accept, or set yourself. But that freedom also brings the responsibility to use your time wisely. Throughout your freelance life, your time is always there to be used productively or wasted, according to the choices you make from day to day.

In this chapter, we'll look at how you can use your time to best effect.

Three time horizons

You need to manage your time over three different horizons.

The first horizon is long-term, and is measured in years, or even decades. This is the grand sweep of your freelance career, leading up to the vision you created in chapter 2. You don't necessarily need to think about it each and every day. But it's worth checking in on it every so often, to reflect on your progress and refocus if you need to. If you keep going in the same direction, will you get to where you want to be? Do you need to change what you're doing – or even rethink your vision?

Checking your long-term progress is a great way to build confidence. When you feel caught up in the busyness of freelance life, take a minute to turn round and look at the road you've travelled so far. Although it can sometimes feel like you're always learning, always a beginner, you've already achieved a great deal.

The second, medium-term horizon is measured in days, weeks and months. This is where you schedule your work, so you know what's coming up and can give clients realistic timescales. You can use pretty much any sort of calendar for this. I use BusyCal on Mac, which combines scheduled events with a day-to-day to-do list. But even a simple printed calendar or diary will do the job.

Get into the habit of keeping track of how long each job takes, so you can learn how to schedule them in future. Remember to include all the 'extras' to the main part of the work, like writing emails, making changes and invoicing. That will give you a very rough sense of how long different tasks take. You can also use this to help you work out prices (see chapter 7).

The third and final time horizon is short-term, and it's measured in hours and days. This is where you decide what you'll do from day to day, and within each day. Referring back to your calendar, decide what you want to achieve by the end of the day, and over the course of the week.

Ordering tasks can be tricky. Sometimes, it's best to launch into that one horrible task you've been dreading, and get it out of the way. But on other days, you just need to do *something* to feel that you've made progress – and sorting out simple admin tasks can be helpful for that. As an introvert, I find that I tend to put off any sort of high-stakes interaction with my clients, such as submitting a price or sending off my first draft once it's ready. Aim for a balance between making headway and preserving headspace – whatever that means for you.

To-do lists are great, but they won't necessarily give any structure to your day. One option is to dedicate certain times of the day to certain tasks.

For example, you could treat email like paper mail: open it in the morning, reply to all the messages right then and there, then quit your mail app until the next day. This could help you avoid being distracted by incoming messages throughout the day. I have a bad habit of reading emails as soon as they arrive, in the hope of quickly dismissing them, only to find that some task or detail mentioned in the email gets stuck in my head and I lose focus on what I was doing before.

Alternatively, you could reward yourself for a hard day's work with a half-hour blast of social media at 5pm. (I use an app called 1Focus, which blocks access to my favourite time-wasting websites at fixed times during the working day.)

Most people find they're more productive at certain times, so aim to do most of your 'real work' when your powers are at their height. I'm at my sharpest in the morning, so if I have some creative writing to do, I try and do it first thing. That can sometimes mean ignoring my inbox until later in the day.

If you've got lots of tasks or projects on the go at the same time, give the pomodoro technique a try. It's a time management technique that can take your natural introvert's concentration and dial it up to 11.

Basically, you make a list of the four or five things you need to work on. You get a simple countdown timer –

your phone will probably do it – and set it for half an hour. You then go into a routine of spending half an hour on the first task, half an hour on the second and so on. You may find you make quicker progress overall, because you're always 'on a deadline', which makes you want to work faster. Also, your subconscious mind is still working while you focus on something else, so you often find that new ideas are waiting when you return to a task.

Taking breaks

Taking breaks is essential. And that applies to all three of the time horizons I discussed just above.

At the daily level, you need breaks within your day so you can relax your eyes, stretch your muscles and give your brain a rest. If you try to sit at your desk all day, you'll gradually lose focus and finish the day feeling exhausted and washed out. So make sure you include movement, changes of scene and non-work activities in every day.

At the weekly/monthly level, you need to take some days off. Although you're theoretically free to have as much time off as you like, you may find it more difficult in practice, particularly once you're a bit busier and clients are clamouring for you to do their work. (There's a section on how to say no in the next chapter.) Even so, you should take at least two 'proper' holidays a year – for example, one during summer and one around Christmas.

There's a strong argument for completely ignoring work when you're on holiday. However, I've found that if I do that, I come back to a mountain of email, including simple enquiries from valued clients that I could have sorted out with a one-line reply. (For example: 'Are you free to do this job next week?' Answer: 'Yes, thank you.') With that in mind, it simply isn't possible to switch off completely, however much fun I might be having. And that can actually end up spoiling the holiday, because of the nagging sense that something might be needing my attention.

To avoid that, I now check my email just once or twice during my holiday. I do it at a specific time – usually the early evening, accompanied by a cold beer. I bin the spam, reassure my regular clients and usually ask new prospects to wait until I get back for their price or proposal. Then I can enjoy the rest of my holiday knowing that everything is OK with my business, and that I'll have work when I get back.

As well as your main holidays, you can throw in a few ad hoc days off during weeks when you're not quite as busy. I find it best to try and complete the week's work by Thursday, and then take Friday off. Go on a shopping spree, a trip to the beach, a walk in the country or whatever feels like a treat to you. You earned this.

The third and final type of break is the longer one, a month or more, that you give yourself when you feel you've made significant progress towards your ultimate goal. To do this, you'll want to feel fully secure in your work, which probably means a broad base of regular clients and a financial cushion too. You might use the time to go travelling, improve your home, learn something new or pursue a personal project, like writing a book.

I can't say too much about this type of break because, even after 15+ years of freelancing, I've yet to make this choice. If you have family who depend on your income, as I do, it's not a decision you can take lightly. However, I have no doubt that it's hugely valuable and worthwhile.

Having said that, I have had a couple of enforced breaks when no work has come in for a week or two. During earlier busy times, I had always told myself that if and when this happened, I would try to embrace it, do something constructive and not just waste the time checking my email and fretting about work picking up again. So when the time came, I did my best – and I'm glad I did, because the break turned out to be shorter than I thought. So if this happens to you, I suggest you do the same.

Time suckers

As we'll see in the next chapter, your introvert listening skills can be a big help with your freelancing. But you also need to make sure no-one takes advantage of them.

Time suckers are people who take up your time without really offering anything in return. Some want to 'pick your brain', which really means getting some free advice. Some claim that they're thinking about using you in the future – but even if they are, it's clearly a long way off. And some just love the sound of their own voice, and want to use you as a sounding board for their own thoughts, ideas and plans. Bizarrely, they will often do this under the pretence of seeking your advice.

In my experience, the most valuable contacts are 'all business'. They're busy, and they want to get stuff done. When they approach you, they're looking for a specific exchange of value, not a sketchy 'relationship'. So they're upfront about what they want to do, and how you can help. It might be work, or it might be an initial discussion, but whatever it is, the proposal will be clear. If they want to meet up socially, they'll say so, and that occasion will be clearly different from a business meeting.

Time suckers, meanwhile, deliberately withhold information to keep things vague, and exploit the power imbalance inherent in the client-freelancer relationship. For example, they might ask to meet for coffee, to 'explore' a hazily defined 'project' or 'opportunity'. Since you're looking for work, you go along, because that's the only way to find out more. But you end up entangled in a meandering discussion about something completely different. Before you know it, you've blown a valuable morning chasing an 'opportunity' that probably doesn't even exist.

There's nothing wrong with meeting potential clients, fellow freelancers or people who sound friendly.

Just learn to tell the genuine approaches from the attempts to steal your time.

Staying focused

The problem with today's workstyle is that our tools are also our toys. In the days before computers, if you were writing on a typewriter, it would never occur to you to suddenly put your feet up and start reading a newspaper. But because your computer offers both those functions in one device, it's all too easy to slip from one to the other, often without even realizing.

However, while it's easy to blame technology for 'distracting us', in reality *we distract ourselves*. We always have a choice of what to do from moment to moment. Technology just gives us the opportunities.

Watch yourself over the course of a working day and notice when you reach for your phone, check your email or log on to social media. You'll probably find it's when you're in particular emotional states – boredom, irritation, anxiety and so on. You use 'distractions' to escape from something you don't want to do, feel or think about at that moment. And even if one means of distraction is out of reach, you'll probably just switch to another.

Learn to recognize your distraction triggers: the tasks you're often doing when you mysteriously start thinking about something else. One of my biggest triggers is sending my work off to clients. It's a high-stakes client interaction and also a point of no return, so

I tend to shy away from it, deferring the moment of truth with pointless busywork or non-work tasks. Another trigger for me is starting a new piece of work, because of the nagging anxiety that I won't be able to do it.

When you hit a trigger, just notice your thoughts, and sit with them for a while until they pass. Some people find it helpful to imagine thoughts as clouds moving across the sky. Then, when you're ready, carry on with your task without resorting to distraction. Tell yourself that it needs doing, and you're going to do it now. You can do the other stuff as a reward for completing it – although you'll probably find that later on, the need will have passed.

Exploring and exploiting

Scholars of business strategy make the distinction between *exploration* and *exploitation*. Exploration is about discovering new innovations, acquiring new skills and developing new products. Exploitation, on the other hand, is about getting full value from the resources you already have. Most firms need to do both in order to survive.

For freelancers, it's about the difference between working *on* your business (exploration) and working *in* it (exploitation). Your business has to develop, but it also has to support you.

Over-exploring generates loads of new ideas that you never finish, so they never make you any money.

Creating new ideas always has an element of play – breaking out of your existing routines so you can create new ones. However, if you play too much, those blue-sky ideas never crystallize into anything useful.

Over-exploiting, meanwhile, means you're stuck in a hamster wheel of day-to-day work. With your head down over your desk, you might miss important new trends that could affect your work, or initiatives you could get involved in. But even if you don't, you may find that you end up feeling stagnant and frustrated, because you're all work and no play. This is a real trap for introverts, who are happy alone and naturally disposed towards losing themselves in their work. Task focus is a positive trait in the right measure, but it can be damaging if taken to excess.

When it comes to time management, it's all about balancing the two sides. You need to 'sharpen the saw' by developing new skills and getting into new areas. But you also need to keep your clients happy and make money, which means using the skills you have right now.

Some freelancers are over-explorers. They're always looking for the next client, relationship, project or event. With no line manager looking over their shoulder, there's nobody to keep them in line. Natural extroverts are more likely to do this, because it means they can go out and meet people instead of sitting down on their own to follow up.

As an introvert, however, you're more likely to over-exploit. Sure, you may *want* to learn new stuff. But exploration can mean putting yourself in new situations with new people. So you shy away from it and stick with what you know instead.

Once you have a few regular clients, it's so easy to tell yourself that you just *have* to exploit. There's always another job to do, and it feels wrong to turn work down. So you end up constantly responding to clients' demands, never setting a new direction of your own.

Of course, your existing clients might ask you to do new things. Once you become their 'go-to guy', many clients would rather stick with you, even for stuff outside your skillset, than risk someone new. But it's still not something you choose for yourself. You're not really exploring; you're just following where your client leads.

Age plays a part too. If you're young and have no dependents, it makes sense to gain new knowledge when your schedule is a little slack. You're making an investment in your future that will mature in the coming years.

On the other hand, the older you get, the harder it is to learn new things – and (without being too morbid) the less time you have left to exploit them. On top of that, freelancers' earning capacity tends to peak in later middle age, before gently declining as we near retirement. So if you've reached a certain 'age and stage' and your inbox is stuffed with work, you might just want to make hay while the sun shines.

Takeaways from this chapter

- Time is your most precious resource. Use it wisely.

- Manage your time over three horizons: years (achieving goals), weeks and months (planning your work) and day-to-day (getting things done).

- Manage your time intelligently by taking breaks, staying focused and avoiding time suckers. Learn how your introversion can affect the way you manage time.

- Balance exploration and exploitation so you can keep developing *and* bring in the cash.

5 *WORKING WITH YOUR CLIENTS*

Love them or hate them, you can't freelance without them. Learn how to work with the clients you need, and avoid the ones you don't.

What makes a good client?

There are certain qualities you'll want to look for in every client. They are:

- They respect you as a person and as a professional

- They give you a clear brief and the space to work on it

- They value the work you do (and ideally praise you for it)

- They treat you fairly and honour their commitments

- They pay on time.

If a client falls short on just one or two of these points, you might be able to grit your teeth and soldier on. If they fail on three or more, the relationship is going to be hard going. Then you'll have to decide whether to try and change the client's behaviour, or just walk away.

Beyond these basic requirements, there's a huge variation in terms of how clients like to work with freelancers. Over time, you'll get to know each of your clients' quirks and foibles, and learn how to anticipate or work around them as necessary.

For example, I have valued clients who diligently check my availability in advance… then blow their own deadline for sending me the work. But I've grown accustomed to that, and learned to work around it. (To be fair, it's often due to circumstances they can't control.)

Your introversion might draw you towards certain clients. For example, you'll probably warm to those who are happy to deal with you in writing, rather than asking for phone calls or meetings – that is, those who are introverts themselves. That, in turn, might mean you wind up with a widely dispersed client base, rather than serving people who are local to you.

Having said that, you may also find that some of your best clients are big-time extroverts who recognize their own limitations. For instance, they might be real go-getters who have no trouble setting ambitious goals and motivating others, but find it harder to refine their ideas, capture their thoughts or follow through on detail. So they'll come to you for abilities and attitudes that complement their own.

Your clients will have their own interaction preferences too. Some will be fully focused on the job, while others will make a point of always asking how you are. Some will thank you effusively for your efforts, while others will forget to say anything until the next time they use you. As long as you know that they value you, it's all good. Compliments are nice – but repeat business is the highest compliment there is.

Before you go freelance, you might think that the relationship between a freelancer and their client is fairly distant and transactional. In reality, you can develop a deep and strong bond with certain clients – at least in some types of work. In fact, you might end up being closer to some of your clients than you are to your fellow freelancers.

The importance of saying no

As we've seen, some clients are better than others. But that's no problem – after all, as a freelancer you can pick and choose your clients, right?

It sounds fine and dandy in theory. But when you come to actually turn work down, you realize how hard it can be. Saying no is a real skill – and one that every freelancer needs to learn.

When someone asks you to do some work, it's like being invited to their party. Obviously, you have a choice. You don't have to do anything you don't want to do. But that doesn't mean that turning them down will be easy or consequence-free.

On one level, deciding which jobs to take on is just about planning your calendar, as we saw in chapter 4. You can't do everything, so you need to prioritize. You also want to work with certain types of client more than others – and there are some you want to avoid altogether (as we'll see below).

However, no matter how strong your rationale may be, saying no rarely feels neutral. It nearly always brings some emotional baggage. And while this will probably lessen over time, it can be a major factor in your early days.

An offer of work can spark a whole bunch of feelings. You may be excited to work with this type of client, or on this type of project. You may be nervous about whether you can deliver – and eager to prove that you can. You may be overawed that a client like this has approached you, and anxious not to let them down. You may be thinking how this job could lead on to other jobs. And, of course, you may be thinking about that money.

However, these feelings can also be a sign that the job is not quite right for you. Maybe it's too far from your core expertise, or beyond your capacity as an individual freelancer. Or maybe you're just too busy to take it on. If you're honest, the client would probably be better off with someone else. And you would be better off doing another job where you can add more value.

If you do decline the job, you abruptly shut all your feelings down, and swap them for others. You may feel loss, regret, guilt or self-reproach. And your inner critic goes fruitloop. That client was ready to pay you cash money... and you *said no!?* They needed your help, and you just *left them hanging?* Who do you think you are? Well, if your business goes down the pan, you've only got yourself to blame.

Obviously, all that stuff is way off base. It's mostly based on wild second-guessing about what the client thinks and feels – which introverts are more prone to. But it still *feels* real to you. It's also worse for you as an introvert, because you don't like making waves or laying down the law. It just isn't in your nature to kick up a fuss.

As a result of all this, saying no – even to just one small job – can feel like stepping off a cliff, or telling an old friend that you never want to see them again. And that means that you can easily end up accepting the work just to avoid the emotional fallout of turning it down.

At the extreme, some freelancers simply say yes to everything, regardless of the consequences, for years on end. They never become the masters of their own careers, preferring the safety of passive acceptance to the risk of taking control. The irony is that, in their eagerness to please, they end up taking on too much, letting people down and ultimately just burning themselves out. Saying no is vital to safeguard your business, the quality of your service and, ultimately, your own wellbeing.

We have a tendency to focus on one bad thing and ignore all the good things.[7] So, to help yourself say no, cultivate a sense of proportion. Remember all the other clients you have, and all the other jobs you've done. Compare the fee for this job to your earnings for the last year, or even your whole freelance career. Remind yourself that there are thousands more clients out there that you can work for. Although this may feel like a huge, irreversible step right now, more work will surely come your way. Every closing is an opening somewhere else.

To counter the sense of loss, focus on what you're *gaining*. You now have the chance to serve other clients better, or do more of the work you really want to do. You can put some time into developing your business. You can spend time on a passion project. Or you can just take some well-earned time off. And most importantly of all, you've gained a real feeling of control and purpose, and the sense of balance in your work and your life. And that brings you more true wealth than any job could ever do.

---

[7] This is called negativity bias. See
https://en.wikipedia.org/wiki/Negativity_bias

Ways to say no

Buyers in a market are not used to providers just turning them down. (Imagine going to a bakery and the owner just flat-out refuses to sell you a loaf.) Saying 'Sorry, I don't want to do this job' is far too blunt. So it helps to give the prospect a different reason for saying no.

Here are a few ideas:

- **You're not a good fit for the project**. It can feel strange saying this when people have actively chosen you, but it can work. Having looked carefully at the brief, you say that they really need a specialist, or a generalist, or someone with more experience, or really anyone else who's different from you in some plausible way. Note that the prospect may be very grateful for this advice, and act on it in good faith. So make it truthful and useful; don't send them on a wild goose chase. If they persist with you, say that you're not confident of meeting their expectations, and you don't want to disappoint them later on. Once you say this, only a pretty ruthless prospect – or an obtuse one – will keep plugging away in the face of your objections.

- **You're too busy**. Nobody can really argue with this. All the prospect can do is offer to wait until you're free – so consider whether you'd want them to. I've seen freelancers claiming to be booked out for the next six months, so you can certainly say something similar.

- **You can't meet their expectations on price**. If you
  quote a price way above the deal zone (see
  chapter 7), one of three things will happen. First,
  the prospect may just give up, which is what you
  wanted anyway. Second, they may ask you to
  revise your price, in which case you just say, 'Sorry,
  but I can't,' effectively ending negotiations.
  However, there's a risk that they might just accept
  the big price, and ratchet up their expectations
  accordingly. As with all pricing, once you commit
  to a price, you lose control – so choose wisely.

The approach you choose depends on the stage of
negotiation you're at. You can't really agree to a project
one day, then claim to be too busy the next. If you're
already into the hands-on work and things are clearly
going south, one option is to offer to invoice half and
walk away with no hard feelings. I've done this several
times with satisfactory results; only one client has
refused to pay anything at all.

When you say no, most clients will accept your reason
and look elsewhere. A few may be puzzled, offended or
even angry. Some may refuse to take no for an answer,
and redouble their efforts to use you. I guess we all
want what we can't have.

As with pricing (chapter 7), it always helps to have the
'conversation' in writing. It's incredibly hard to express
a tactful rejection over the phone – let alone face to face.
What's more, the client's reaction is completely
unpredictable, so you don't know where you'll end up.
(If you do put your foot in it, send an email later on

clarifying your reasons, and admitting you find phone calls difficult.)

Whatever angle you take, be courteous and professional throughout, taking responsibility for the situation yourself. Normally, taking on blame would be bad for the future relationship – but in this case, you probably don't want one anyway, so it's fine to act out your part and move on.

Rogue clients and how to spot them

In the early stages of your career, you may feel that you have to take every job, whether for financial reasons or just to build up your skills and experience. However, some clients are so difficult to work with that their projects are simply not worth taking on. The negative experience will spill over to affect your other work, to the point where the money you earn is outweighed by the emotional cost.

It's hardly surprising when you think about it. You're putting yourself out there as a provider who literally *anyone* can use. You work with people who are complete strangers to you – yet everything depends on how well you can communicate and collaborate. Inevitably, some of the resulting relationships will go wrong. (To be honest, it's amazing how many of them go *right*.)

It's easy to tell when a live project is going off the rails. But by then, it's too late. You need to spot rogue clients *before* you jump into bed with them.

Some red flags include:

- **Looking for freebies**. People may say things like, 'There's lots more work in the pipeline,' or, 'We just need to see what you can do.' Even if the claims are true (which is a big if), this tactic still doesn't bode well for the future relationship. (We'll come back to working for free in chapter 7.)

- **Pushing for a lower price**. If my trusted clients do this, it's no problem. I tell them what I can offer and we go from there. But if a new prospect tries it, it sours the relationship right from the get-go. I'm thinking, 'If you're like this now, what will you be like once we get into the project?' Asking for discounts is often a power play: the whole point is that they demand, and you comply. The price you pay to win the work is psychological as well as financial.

- **Saying there's no budget**. Since the client's finances are none of your concern, this is an attempt to make you bow to a higher authority: the all-powerful budget. Personally, I'd rather people just came out and asked for a price cut, instead of pointing to a budget that may be arbitrary or indeed non-existent.

- Just generally **dwelling on the price**, or what they get for it, without directly asking you to reduce it. For example, 'Wow! For £1500, I'm looking forward to some fantastic results.' It *sounds* like a compliment, but it could also be a veiled threat, or a sign that your work will never satisfy.

True professionals shake hands on the price, then never mention it again.

- Trying to **change the basis for payment**, possibly after it's been agreed. For example, they might try to switch from per-project to per-hour, or even some sort of 'no result, no fee' deal. Unless 'result' depends on a fair, objective measure that you fully understand and agree to, you should steer well clear. Don't let your livelihood become a hostage to fortune.

- **Asking how much they can get** for a certain price, or a certain number of hours. For example, 'What could you do for £100?' You simply cannot build a respectful, professional relationship from a beginning like this. If they're asking this question, they really need to use someone cheaper. Politely tell them so.

- **Being pushy about timescales** – and getting defensive when you push back. For example, expecting you to respond to their emails in minutes, while yours go unanswered for weeks. (Having said that, some valuable clients *always* ask for quick delivery, but still accept your timescales with good grace. You have to decide where to draw the line.)

- **An unclear brief.** If the client doesn't know what they want, how can you deliver it? Setting off without a map just stores up problems for later on. Plus the lazy thinking shows disrespect in itself. (It's also irritating when clients belatedly reveal information that they should have conveyed up front, but this can sometimes be an honest mistake. Again, you must make the judgement.)

- **Over-fussiness**. Obviously, clients have a right to expect a certain level of quality, and to request changes when you've missed the mark. What they *can't* do is send you on a wild goose chase for an unachievable goal, saying 'I'll know it when I see it' and revising the brief on the fly at every turn. Say up front what changes are included in your price, and stick to your guns.

- **Disregarding your advice**. Why would anyone buy a dog and bark themselves? There's often scope for a constructive discussion of the reasoning behind your suggestions. But simply ignoring your advice is something else. It's not your job to justify something that the client is going to do anyway. And if things go wrong later on, who will be responsible?

- **Renegotiation after the fact**. This can involve sneaking in more elements after the price is agreed, or getting extra bits done under the guise of making amendments. 'Feature creep' (or 'scope creep') is hard to deal with because you want to be accommodating, and it's up to you to come out and say 'enough is enough'. There's a risk of looking 'difficult' (a classic misconception about introverts) when you're actually just sticking to the deal.

- Trying to **get you on the back foot**. Phone calls at strange times or unusual, unexpected requests can be a tactic to throw you off balance and extract concessions. For you as an introvert, a client constantly phoning when you clearly prefer email is another way to tip the power balance. Thank heavens for caller display.

- **Passive aggression.** For example, putting words in your mouth to make you feel that you've been critical or over-demanding, when in fact you've been perfectly professional. It's almost impossible to call out, and you may wonder if it's even really happening. Believe me, it is – and it can drive you crazy.

- **Creepy behaviour.** Inappropriate comments, intrusive personal questions, unwanted touching and anything else that makes you feel uneasy has absolutely no place in a professional working relationship. You are fully justified in ending the association immediately, and by any means necessary. No fee is worth this.

- **Time-sucking** (see chapter 4). Unless you are charging by the hour for it, you don't want your clients to use you as a chat line or a counselling service. Some clients love having a friendly, impartial outsider to moan to or gossip with – but you have to keep a lid on it, or you risk wasting your most precious resource. Learn to make the distinction between a friendly chat and professional consultancy or advice.

- **Late or non-payment** (see chapter 7). Obviously, if you get this far, you've already committed to the project. But if you have to chase for payment, or if you hear a lot of implausible excuses along the way, you probably won't want to take on any more work for the client.

Despite this long list, it's hard to say for sure what you should look for. You might even have a client who does one or more of these things, but you're totally happy with it. I've even heard tales of relationships that became stronger after the supplier sued the client for non-payment. The crucial question is whether you feel the client is acting in good faith, or just trying to gain power over you.

In the end, spotting rogue clients is more of a *feeling* than a finding. Sometimes you get that feeling just from a word, a gesture, a tone of voice. You just *know*. And when you get that feeling, *trust it*.

Now, this can be difficult for an introvert, because you've become accustomed to overriding your own unease or discomfort in a whole range of situations involving other people. It's part of the emotional labour that falls on introverts' shoulders, which we saw in chapter 1. You may also have problems setting boundaries, or telling other people what you want. But in this case, it's vital that you listen to your emotions and act on them.

Tune into your true feelings about the future of this project, or this client relationship. Never mind how much you want the work, or the money. If this job goes ahead, how will you actually feel? Being totally honest, would you be relieved if it *didn't* go ahead? How much money would make it OK? Or, when you think about it, is the money actually beside the point?

Just as the good character of your best clients comes through in all their dealings with you, so shiftiness is always there, just beneath the surface. So when people show you who they are, believe them. Over time, you'll get better at spotting bad apples, and at trusting your own intuition too.

I don't want to suggest that the world is full of wicked clients who are out to destroy you. It isn't. You can safely freelance for clients of all types and all personalities, all over the world. It's just that a few negative experiences can really stick in your memory, and colour your feelings about your whole freelance career. That, in turn, affects your future choices, which affect your future success. So it's worth being prepared, and having some strategies ready for when your spidey-sense starts tingling.

Listening to your clients

As an introvert, you're a natural listener, and that will help you a lot in your freelance career.

First and foremost, at a practical level, listening helps you find out what clients want from a project.
It also gives a good balance between learning and actively contributing – the less you say, the more telling and memorable it is when you *do* speak. And on the softer side, listening helps you build a stronger

relationship with clients, because it shows understanding and respect.

Interviewing clients is an indispensable skill in my line of work, writing. But every freelancer can benefit from it. It's a really useful way to gather information about the project that will help you avoid mistakes and misunderstandings later on.

What makes the difference between shooting the breeze and an interview? In a word, preparation. First, you arrange a specific time for your discussion, and agree how you'll carry it out (in person, phone, Skype etc). In good time before the interview, you prepare a list of questions and share it with the client – not as a rigid script to follow, but just as a general guide to the themes that the conversation needs to cover. You also set up some method of recording the interview, whether that's an audio recorder on your phone or computer, or just a pen and paper.

Some useful questions to get clients talking are:

- What is this project all about? What is the goal?

- Who is the project for, and how will it help them?

- What does success look like? How will we know when we've succeeded?

- How can I help? What can I bring to this project?

You might be surprised at where these questions take you, or the things that the client has not yet thought about. But it's hard to develop an idea on your own. That's why clients really appreciate the chance to talk things over with someone else. In fact, that might even be the most valuable thing you offer them – which is fine, as long as you're paid for your time, and they don't become a time sucker (chapter 4).

Notice that most of these are open questions, beginning 'how' or 'what'. They invite answers that are descriptive or narrative, so the client can explore their own thoughts. 'Why' questions, or those with yes/no answers, tend to be more useful for tying up loose ends, closing off options or resolving uncertainty.

Freelancing is about fitting your own skills and knowledge to the needs of the client. So as you listen to them speak, it's only natural that your thoughts turn to how you could help them, or how you'd approach their project. The problem is that once you fall into that mindset, you're no longer listening, but thinking of what you could say. That raises the risk that you leap into the conversation with your own half-formed ideas, and disrupt the client's flow.

Or you may have nothing in particular to say, but still get lost in your own self-consciousness or anxiety, and realize with a start that you've disappeared inside your own head.

To avoid those traps, cultivate the skill of *active listening*. When you listen actively, you concentrate all your effort on understanding, learning and remembering what the other person says. You relax control over the conversation, while still guiding it with questions when required. You let go of your judgement and evaluation until they are actually needed or requested. And you accept that your own ideas or beliefs might be changed by what you hear.[8]

Preconceptions can be powerful. I've often found that when I listen back to an interview recording, the client is saying something quite different from what I thought at the time. I then have to listen to myself asking stupid, beside-the-point questions on the recording, which is excruciating. But I can deal with it, as long as I get the information I need in the end.

Hearing clients isn't the same as understanding them. Sometimes, they may seem to be saying one thing, but they really mean something else. For example, if the client is explaining what they want from a project, they might use words like 'modern' or 'informal' that *seem* clear, but when you dig deeper, are actually quite hard to pin down, or support multiple meanings. So it's often worth asking clients to provide real-world examples of what they want, and encouraging them to say what *specifically* they like about them.

Cut your clients some slack. Bear in mind that they may never have used a service like yours before, or worked with a freelancer of any kind. Also, if they are running a startup business, remember that they may be paying for your work with their own savings, which they earned from their own work. They're probably keen, if not desperate, for this project to work out well.

---

[8] Learn more about active listening at
https://en.wikipedia.org/wiki/Active_listening

That can easily manifest in behaviours that, from your side, can seem nit-picky or over-controlling.

From this perspective, it's clear that listening isn't just about gathering information. It's also about gauging your client's mood, and picking up on any anxieties or preoccupations they may have. If they keep on repeating particular points, or returning to a particular theme, that's a strong signal that they're concerned about something. If they reveal what went wrong with a previous project, they're really saying what they want to go right this time round.

Their body language can also provide clues, which is why meeting a client in person often helps you build a stronger rapport than dealing over email or by phone. Although you may have to fight through your own discomfort, it could be worth it long-term. I've often found that just one meeting with a client makes a substantial and permanent improvement to the quality of the relationship from then on. Love it or hate it (and we introverts hate it), there's nothing quite like meeting somebody face to face.

A special case of listening is the meeting or group call where people on the client side have different views that affect the project. For instance, you may get on a briefing call, only to discover that the managing director, marketing director and production director have not yet agreed what this project is all about. It's frustrating, but there's no escape now. So use the time to listen to everyone and work out what it means for you. Who actually has authority here, and what is your relationship with them? Who has information that you need? Who's going to approve your work? Then use the answers to decide how you'll approach the project.

Under-promise and over-deliver

As a general rule, let your work do the talking. It's far better to under-promise and over-deliver than to promise the moon on a stick and come up short.

You want to instil confidence in the client, but without over-inflating expectations. This modest, understated stance feels totally natural to introverts, so it should come easy. (Just don't take it so far that you start actively talking down your own abilities.)

If clients ask what you can bring to a job, say that you'll do your best to meet the brief, to the best of your abilities. If they ask about end results, say that you'll aim to improve on what they have at the moment. Instead of making big claims about what you can do, just point to what you've done before, and what other clients have said about you (see 'Testimonials' in chapter 6).

When it comes to timescales, give a worst case and say that you'll do your best to improve on it. This is far better than committing to a quick turnaround, giving yourself a load of stress and still letting the client down at the end of it.

I *always* give worst-case delivery dates, even if I'm 99% sure that I'll beat them by days. Maybe clients see through this trick, but I still don't think they mind.

An artificially long deadline that you never break is still *far* better than an insanely short one that you invariably crash through.

When clients move on

We've looked at how to say no to a client or project you don't want. But what about when you lose a client you really wanted to keep?

This is a tough situation for introverts, because we often prefer just a few deep relationships to lots of shallow ones. For example, we'll make a few close friends, and tend to stick with them over the long term. So 'breaking up' with a client comes particularly hard for us. And it pays to be prepared.

The first thing to remember is that the client's decision might be nothing to do with you. For example, it could be because they have fewer resources to spare, or because their business is going in a different direction. Or they might be looking for someone to help them chase some new fad or fashion. That doesn't mean your service is bad or obsolete – just that it it's no longer right for this particular client.

Sometimes, clients just feel like a change. Again, there's not a lot you can do; it's just a natural human impulse to switch things up from time to time. You've done your best to meet the client's expectations, but perhaps your work for them has become a bit predictable. Maybe you would also benefit from a change.

For many clients, the whole point of using freelancers is the freedom to build a flexible team and choose horses for courses. That has two sides: it can bring you new clients, as well as taking old ones away.

I've found that many clients use my service just once, and never come back. I don't think they're dissatisfied – indeed, many have given me positive reviews. Maybe they really just needed that one job. Or maybe it's just the nature of the freelance market that encourages people to shop around.

Whatever the reason, remember that there are plenty more fish in the sea. Unless your ideal client profile (chapter 2) is incredibly restrictive, there are loads more clients out there who will be right for you – perhaps even better than the client who just left.

Yes, you've lost a client. But you haven't lost your ability to gain clients, or to do great work. Your offer is still just as strong today as it was yesterday.

The key is to *go where you give value*. There's no point chasing work that isn't right for both parties.
If you can't add value for one client, find another one for whom you can.

Takeaways from this chapter

- Some clients are more valuable, and more valued, than others.

- Saying no is a vital way to prevent burnout and safeguard the quality of your work.

- Learn to spot rogue clients early, and say no *before* you get entangled with them.

- Use your introvert's listening skills to manage projects and build strong client relationships.

- A reliable freelancer is like gold dust, so always under-promise and over-deliver.

- When clients move on, let them go – however hard you find it as an introvert. Focus on going wherever you can give the most value.

6 *MARKETING YOURSELF*

Self-promotion may not come easy to introverts,
but it's an essential part of freelancing.

Why you need marketing (even though you hate it)

Freelance introverts often find marketing tough.
It's usually because they think of it as 'arrogance',
'boasting', 'egotism' or something like that.
When you're a natural wallflower, blowing your
own trumpet just feels… wrong.

Unfortunately, there's no way round it. Unless you're
remarkably lucky with word-of-mouth referrals from
people you already know, you will have to market
yourself. So you're going to have to toughen up and get
used to self-promotion.

Some freelancers kid themselves that marketing is some
sort of optional extra – something they fit in as and
when, if they don't have any real work to do that day.

It's better to think of marketing as *generating future cash flow*. Your actions today determine your success tomorrow. The sooner you get down to it, the sooner you'll see the benefit.

Another reason for marketing is that it determines what clients think of you *before* they get in touch. The more positive their impressions of you, the higher the deal zone (chapter 7) will reach. In other words, the stronger your freelance brand, the more you can charge.

Ways to find new clients

When you first start freelancing, building a client base can seem truly daunting. How will you find new clients? How will they find you? How do you actually get from having no clients at all to supporting yourself with freelance work?

Before you start, accept that your journey will probably take a little time. You will have to go step by step, and each step you take will show the way for the next one. But remember that *everything* you try will bring some sort of learning, progress and reward. It might not actually win you any business right there and then, but it will still help you.

Everybody's story of freelance success is unique, and if you ask another freelancer how they got started, you may be surprised at how different their journey has been from yours. But at the same time, there are usually certain common approaches that everybody tries, at some time and to some extent.

Your options for finding new clients are:

- Working for **people you already know** from previous jobs, friendships, family links and so on

- Getting **referrals from existing clients**, where they recommend you to someone they know

- Getting **referrals from other freelancers** who have too much work (where they pass the contact over to you, and you deal with the client direct)

- Getting **subcontracted work from other freelancers** (where they retain direct contact with the client)

- **Partnering with other freelancers** who have complementary skills and can bring in clients for both of you – for example, a web designer and a back-end website developer working as a team

- Working with a **firm or agency** who need your skills to support their own offering – a digital agency, a PR agency, a marketing agency, a law firm and so on

- Getting **new enquiries** from visitors to your own website

- **Driving more traffic** to your website through link-building or advertising (like Google AdWords)

- Getting yourself listed in an **online directory** where people can read about your skills and / or link to your website to find out more

- **Cold calling**, where you make phone calls to introduce yourself to people who've never worked with you before

- **Direct marketing**, where you use email or paper letters to introduce yourself to prospects

- **Networking**, where you attend organized events like fairs and conferences to meet new contacts who could potentially give you work

- **Sharing your work, thoughts or expertise**, mainly through social media, to build your profile and reputation and ultimately attract more clients

- **Traditional advertising** in printed media like newspapers or magazines, or even radio or TV.

The rest of this chapter looks at how to use these channels, focusing in particular on the ones that are most likely to work well for you as an introvert.

Creating your marketing mix

Obviously, you can't use every marketing channel listed above. But then, you wouldn't want to – for several reasons.

Firstly, you have limited resources, and you want to invest them where they'll have the greatest effect. Resources include time, motivation and goodwill, as well as money. All are precious, and none should be wasted.

Secondly, some channels will be more effective for you than others. For example, a listing in a highly relevant directory may bring you just a handful of clients – yet it could still pay for itself many times over, if those clients stay with you long-term. In contrast, a newspaper ad, while it may feel like it's 'getting you out there', may not actually reach that many of your ideal clients at all.

As a general principle, invest in targeting rather than sheer exposure. Focus on converting your most likely prospects, not casting the net as wide as you can. Remember, you only need a few good clients – loyal ones, who bring you lots of work plus referrals – to build a viable freelance business. And that's good for you as an introvert, because you naturally tend towards cultivating a small and select group of clients.

Thirdly, using some channels may require certain skills, and learning those skills may involve some time or cost. For example, there's a real art to creating effective Google or Facebook ads. However, once you know how, it doesn't take that long to knock up a new one.

Fourthly, respect your introversion. There will be marketing activities you really enjoy (like, say, blogging) and things that bring you out in a cold sweat (like cold calling). If you build your marketing strategy around the second type of task, you're not going to get very far. You'll do a few tasks in a random, half-hearted way, then start finding reasons not to. Before long, you'll be dreading your marketing, putting it off and thinking of it as a major challenge – which it really doesn't need to be.

So, if you enjoy a marketing task, do it. On the other hand, if you have to force yourself to do it, and it never feels natural to you, try and find something else to do instead. Ideally, the alternative will give you the same sort of result, but without the hassle or the heartache.

To sum up, here are the points to consider for each marketing channel:

- Will it reach the right people? If so, how many?
- Will you enjoy doing it?
- Will you be able to sustain it?
- What will you have to invest – in terms of time, money or anything else?
- Taking all these things into account, is this channel right for you?

By considering all these points, you can arrive at your individual marketing mix: a set of activities that you can commit to doing as part of your weekly routine. As with all your plans, it will be more likely to come true if you write it down.

For example, you might decide to:

- Write a customized approach letter to one new prospect every week
- Post two LinkedIn updates every week
- Blog about an industry development once a month
- Follow five new freelancers or industry thought leaders on social media every week

- Request a testimonial at the end of every job.

Whatever marketing mix you choose, it has to be sustainable. In other words, you need to be sure that you'll have enough time and motivation to keep on doing it. Marketing is a bit like diet or exercise: it's a *process*, not a one-off task. You can't get it out of the way in one massive splurge, because you need it to bring you new business continuously over time.

Aim to do one small thing every day, or every week, to promote yourself. It's easier emotionally, and it will give you a real feeling of progress. It will also get you into the habit of talking about yourself, so you can overcome your natural modesty and reticence about self-promotion. As Confucius said, 'It doesn't matter how slowly you go, as long as you do not stop.'

Write your personal pitch

As we saw in chapter 2, the words you use to describe yourself and your future are very powerful, because they shape your expectations of what you can achieve.

Now it's time to decide how you'll describe yourself to others, by writing your personal pitch. Your pitch will shape prospects' perceptions of how you can help them, and what you'll be like to work with. It will also form the basis of all your marketing content.

To write your pitch, go back to the things you considered in chapter 2 – your skills, your target clients, your values, your aims and your story. Now, make them 'face outwards' towards your ideal prospects.

Say what you are (your freelance 'job title'), what you do, who you do it for and how you can help them. For example:

> *I'm a freelance web developer who builds beautiful, hardworking websites for small business owners. If you want to reach new customers and make sales online, I can help. I believe every organization can benefit from great design, and I want to use my skill to help your business succeed.*

Read your pitch out loud to yourself. It might feel slightly awkward and unfamiliar, but that's fine – you'll get used to talking about yourself this way. If it feels unbearably pretentious, and you really can't imagine saying it to anyone else, you'll probably want to tone it down.

If you're in need of some inspiration, head over to LinkedIn. Every profile includes a job title and a longer bio. Read what others like you have done, and see if it sparks your own ideas.

Many freelancers on LinkedIn frame their offer in terms of *how they help*, rather than what they do. For example, they might give their 'job title' as 'Helping small businesses discover the potential of blockchain.' That's fine if it works for you, but bear in mind that people may search for you using terms that are more familiar to them. If someone's looking for a window cleaner, you may not want to say that you're 'Helping office workers keep their spaces clean and light' –

no matter how wonderful it may sound. People can only use your service once they've found it.

Do you need a personal brand?

A brand is the sum of all the thoughts that people have about a product or organization. So in a sense, every freelancer has a brand, because their clients and prospects will inevitably form some impression of them, and hold it in their minds.

Personal branding is about deliberately shaping that impression. You can do it by giving yourself a more distinctive title (like 'The Superlative Sales Trainer'), incorporating as a business or creating a visual identity. Some freelancers even create a cartoon character or Memoji version of themselves, which acts as their avatar on social media.

When you brand yourself, you go from being a person in a category (like 'a photographer') to something more unique (like 'The Business Portrait Specialist'). That's the power of brands – they promise something you can't get anywhere else. If you want the taste of a Coke, or the sound of a Harley-Davidson, you have to get the real thing.

Personal branding has both pros and cons. When you're an introvert, it can be helpful to put some distance between yourself and your business. You create a character or a brand outside yourself, and it can go places, say things and do things that you can't – or at least, that you prefer not to. It's like a mask you wear, or a puppet you control. Separating yourself and your work in this way can also make it easier to deal with challenges or criticism, because they relate to your business, not you.

On the downside, creating and maintaining a brand is a long-term commitment, and it takes time and effort. Also, you might feel that it's all rather artificial, and that you'd rather be 'just yourself'. At the end of the day, whatever brand you build should be an asset, not a hassle.

'I' or 'we'?

If you're an introvert who's not used to self-promotion, working on things like your personal pitch can be excruciating. You're naturally modest and self-effacing, preferring to blend in rather than stand out. But here you are going on and on about yourself, saying 'I this' and 'I that' over and over again.

To some extent, you just have to live with that. Being a freelancer means being able to speak about yourself, clearly and confidently. At the very least, you need to be able to answer a question like 'Tell me about yourself and your work' when first meeting a client. That's why preparing a personal pitch is useful.

At other times, however, there is another option. Instead of positioning yourself as an individual, you can choose a business name and present yourself as a company. That gives you the option of saying 'we' instead of 'I' when speaking or writing about yourself.

Of course, the underlying reality hasn't changed. You're still just one person. But this small change of positioning can make a big difference to your mindset. Because you're talking about 'your company', not just yourself, you're free to be far more expansive about your abilities, experience and clients. That, in turn, can make more of a positive impression on clients.

Becoming 'we' might also help if you do several different things. You may well be competent to deliver them all, but prospects might still be suspicious that a 'jack of all trades' is master of none. But a company that offers a wide range of services might make more sense.

The most obvious place to say 'we' is in marketing material, like your website, and maybe on social media. You *can* keep it up when you meet clients in person, although you may find that awkward when you start discussing practicalities. They may even ask you outright: 'Is the business just you?' If so, honesty is the best policy. In my experience, no-one will think less of you just for presenting yourself as a firm. In fact, they're more likely to be impressed by your ambition and self-confidence.

You don't necessarily have to actually incorporate as a business – you could just use a trading name as a 'front' for self-employment. However, becoming a company does bring many advantages, not least in terms of how you manage your money. On the psychological side, it can be helpful to have a clear dividing line between you and your business. Freelance work has a strong tendency to spill over into personal life as it is; when you form a company, you have more of a sense of your work being 'in its box' (see 'Setting boundaries' in chapter 3). And of course, having a company means the way is open if you do decide to expand, and employ other people.

Your website

Every freelancer needs a website. It's the public face of your freelance business, and it's how most clients will learn about you before they get in touch. It also allows them to find you through search engines.

Websites are a gift for introverts. Before they existed, you'd have to hustle for all your work in person, by mail or on the phone. (Can you imagine?) Now, you can just sit back and let the website do the talking for you. However, that does mean you need to get your website right, so it will actually convert visitors into clients.

So, what should you say on your site?

You should definitely cover these areas:

- **What you do**: the services you offer your clients, and the type of projects you work on

- **Who you work for**: what types clients you serve (individuals, small firms, larger firms; business-to-consumer or business-to-business; specific industries), and in which locations (local, national, international)

- **Your work**: examples of things you've done that showcase your skills (from previous roles, if necessary). These can form an actual portfolio of work, case studies where you just describe what you did, or a combination of both

- **What clients say**: testimonials from clients if you have them (see below), or maybe endorsements from former colleagues or other contacts if you don't

- **About you**: a brief bio, focusing mainly on relevant work experience, and including a photo portrait (helpful when meeting people for the first time)

- **Contact**: details of how to get in touch, which can include a contact form, email address, phone numbers, your business address and perhaps a map showing how to get there

- **Terms and conditions**: details of how you handle formal aspects like project scope, scheduling, invoicing, payment, intellectual property, final approval and so on (you can link here when submitting proposals)

- **Calls to action**: bits of text, probably visible on each page, encouraging visitors to take the next step and actually contact you.

Other areas you might want to cover are:

- **Prices**: sample prices for some typical types of project, or preset packages that you offer (see chapter 7 for more on this)

- **Approach**: a description of your working method, or the values you bring to your work

- **News**: details of important changes, events, projects, client wins and so on (only add this if you're prepared to keep it fresh with updates)

- **Blog posts**: articles on projects, ideas, reflections, techniques, experiences and anything else you want to share (see 'Sharing your thoughts' below).

Your site needs to describe what you do fully and accurately, and give some sense of what you're like to work with. However, your goal is not to tell visitors your life story, but to make them get in touch, right now. The content and design you choose should all work towards that aim.

Many B2B websites end up looking and feeling broadly similar. For example, the links in the navigation are all along the lines of the items in the lists above ('What we do', 'About us', etc). As a copywriter myself, I feel that's OK. Visitors are busy businesspeople who are in the market for a service. You don't really gain anything by using intriguing language or unfamiliar navigation that just puts obstacles in their way.

When it comes to design, you can't go wrong with something simple and clean. However, if your work is more visual – or if you are actually a web designer – you might want something with more impact.

The quickest and easiest way to create a website is with a preset theme in Wordpress, or a site-building platform like Squarespace. However, you might find the cookie-cutter designs a bit limiting, in which case you need a web designer/developer to create a site for you. This needn't be too expensive, if they are also freelance. If they themselves use something like Wordpress, you should be able to update your site yourself – but make sure you mention up front that you want to do this.

If you just want to create a portfolio, you can use platforms like Contently (for writing) or Tumblr or Pinterest (for images). You can also add projects and documents to your LinkedIn profile. This could be a valuable stopgap until you're ready to build your own site.

Testimonials

Testimonials are very powerful because they offer an impartial review of what you do. Prospects can read what somebody like them thinks of your work: if you helped that other client, you can probably help them too. And most importantly, clients will say things in testimonials that you might be too modest to say about yourself – or might never think of saying at all.

All testimonials are worth having, but some are more valuable than others. Ideally, you want a set of quotes that come together to highlight all the important aspects of your service – your skills, your reliability, your working approach and so on. With some clients, you may be able to indicate the sort of things you'd like them to say. When it comes to choosing testimonials to feature, aim to select and edit them to give an overall balance, rather than just including anything and everything.

Wait. Editing your testimonials? Is that really OK? Yes, I think so – as long as the client would still recognize their own thoughts. Your clients may not be accomplished writers, plus they will not spend hours polishing their quote when they're only doing it as a favour to you. So I think it's fine to take out waffle, repetition or unwanted description. Aim for something really punchy and powerful, like the quotes you see on paperbacks: 'Excellent work', 'Would definitely recommend', and so on.

You can strengthen the credibility of your testimonials by hosting them at a third-party website, where you can't control who posts a review, or what they say.[9] You can also request endorsements on LinkedIn. However, the downside is that you can't edit the quotes in the way I've just described. So you might still want to put edited versions on your own site too.

Networking

If an evil genius sat down to design a way to torture introverts, they'd probably come up with something very like a business networking event.

Travelling to an unfamiliar location. Being in a crowd. Meeting strangers. Talking about yourself. Hearing

---

[9] See my own reviews at FreeIndex: https://www.freeindex.co.uk/profile(abc-copywriting)_117528.htm. This site also allows reviews to be integrated into your own site.

them talk about *them*selves. And doing it all with the awful feeling that you *have* to make this work, or your business will never grow.

Well, the good news is that you can easily build a thriving freelance business without going anywhere near a networking event, if you want to. In more than 15 years as a freelancer, I've been to just three. (And one of those was because a 'prospect' inveigled me into going.)

So, why would you go? Well, because it *can* help to grow your business – but perhaps not as immediately as you hope.

The truth is that very few people go to networking events to find service providers. If they really want something done, they do what you and I do: they Google it. So you probably won't walk out of that business brunch with half a dozen hot leads under your arm. However, that doesn't mean networking is a complete waste of time.

First, you might still make contact with someone who might use you at some point in the future. And that's definitely a contact worth making. In fact, it's much more relaxing to meet a prospect this way, without feeling any pressure to close a deal right there and then.

Second, you might expand your network, which might bring you some business indirectly, through referral. It's impossible to tell which seeds will grow, or when. But the more contacts you have, the more likely it is.

And if nothing else, you might meet someone you'd happily go for coffee and a chat with.

However, set against those benefits is the cost of going to the event itself. There may be the financial cost of travelling and admission. There's *definitely* the opportunity cost of spending time you could use for something else. And finally, there's the emotional cost of putting yourself through the experience: you might spend so long feeling anxious about going that it simply isn't worth it.

This is particularly likely if you have to speak to a group, but just walking into a room full of strangers, and having to introduce yourself, can be stressful enough. Even if you just stand in the corner saying nothing, you'll be beating yourself up for not doing it right or wasting your own time. While the physical effort required is negligible, the emotional labour involved in networking, for an introvert, is immense.

To make it easier on yourself, be sure to write your personal pitch, discussed above. Having this in mind will really help if someone asks about what you do. By preparing your pitch in advance, you create a shield that will protect you in your interactions, and set limits on what you want to reveal. The last thing you want is to end up floundering, over-talking or clamming up, just because you're too flustered in the moment to say the right thing.

Be yourself. Don't try to act extrovert just because you feel you should, or because the occasion demands it.

If you're looking to build future relationships, there's no point in giving people a false impression of what you would be like to work with. Instead, go with the flow – use your introvert strengths to get the most out of the event in a way that works for you.

The easiest way to take the pressure off is to ask people questions, and listen carefully to the answers. (We focused on listening in chapter 5.) Most professionals will be hugely flattered if you ask them about their work, or (even better) seek their advice or opinion, and will happily fill many minutes with their response. What's more, they'll remember you as someone really thoughtful and intelligent – even though you only said about five words. Just imagine they have a big sign above their head saying 'Make me feel important'.

Going with someone else can be a big help. Try to recruit a fellow introvert, so they'll relate to your anxiety and stick with you at the event (instead of immediately abandoning you and going off to mingle).

Don't feel you have to stay for the whole event. If you feel yourself tiring, make an excuse (if you need to) and retreat. And however long you stay, give yourself time afterwards to recharge your introvert batteries with some much-needed solitude.

Direct marketing

'Snail mail' can feel hopelessly old-fashioned in the age of social media, but it still works. That's why plenty of companies are still sending out the direct mailshots that drop through your letterbox. There's something about a physical envelope, personally addressed, that's hard to resist.

A letter to an individual feels selective and intimate, which can suit introverts. It says that you don't want to talk to just anyone. You've selected that specific person to receive your message, you've chosen your words carefully and you really care about the response. An email is not quite the same, but it can still have a similar effect, as long as it's framed as a personal communication and not an indiscriminate mailshot.

Don't just spam every company who might use your services. Instead, choose those who are most likely to use you. Go to the trouble of finding out the name and address of the person you need to write to, instead of firing off your message and hoping (or requesting) that it will get forwarded on.

In your letter, be specific: explain why you *specifically* are right for that firm *specifically*. In fact, make your letter as much about 'you' as it is about 'I'. That's far more persuasive than saying 'Here I am, got any work?' It also reflects the listening, responsive mindset that you bring to your freelance work (see chapter 5).

Should you follow up letters with a call, and maybe try to set up a meeting straight away? Some would say so, but I'm not sure. Even if people like the look of you, they probably won't have a suitable project right there and then. A follow-up letter or call later on, to jog their memory, may be more effective. To furnish a reason for the follow-up, you can say something like 'I've got some free time for new projects, and I wondered if you needed help with anything.'

Sharing your work

For many freelance introverts, it's all about the work. They hate being in the spotlight themselves. Instead, they want *the things they create* to go out into the world and engage with people on their behalf. That could mean actual creative work, or it could mean practical solutions to clients' problems.

Luckily, sharing your work is an excellent method of self-promotion. Instead of talking about yourself – which you hate – you simply show people the results they can expect from you.

If you do creative work, it's never been easier to share the fruits of your labours through all the digital channels available today. If you're a writer, there's Twitter, Medium and so on. For visual work, you can share images on Tumblr, Flickr or Pinterest, or build a portfolio on Carbonmade. And Facebook works for pretty much everybody.

If you can't show people your work directly, you can tell them about it instead, by writing and sharing case studies about projects you've worked on. Make sure you cover:

- Who the client is, and what they do
- What they needed from the project

- The problem that the project aimed to solve

- What you did, and how you solved the problem

- The results that the client obtained.

When you use this kind of structure, your case study will naturally fall into a story format. The beginning is the client and their problem, the middle is what you did on the project and the end is the results.

You can also include a testimonial (see above) from the client in your case study. It could cover any of the points above, but ideally the results they saw from your work. Instead of just tacking on a massive quote at the end, see if you can weave shorter quotes throughout the narrative, so the client's words form part of the story as it unfolds. To see how to do this, look at novels or newspaper reports rather than business marketing.

Most clients won't mind you sharing what you've done for them – after all, it's free publicity for them. However, you may still want to just get their permission before you go public. Agencies, in particular, don't always want to admit that they rely on freelance support to provide their 'full-service' offering.

Sharing your thoughts

Sharing your thoughts and opinions is a great way to build up your public profile and reputation as an expert. You can write about your own work, but it doesn't have to end there. Potential subjects include:

- Reflections on your work, or projects you've worked on

- Advice, how-to guides, handy tips and dos and don'ts

- Interviews with other people in your industry

- Your opinions on events, changes and trends in your industry

- Your reviews or analyses of other work in your industry.

All these types of project have the side benefit of promoting your own learning. For example, analyzing other people's work pushes you to sharpen up your thoughts on what does and doesn't work. Instead of just saying you like it (or don't), you have to say why.

Once upon a time, I would have recommended doing this on your own blog. However, in recent years, blogging platforms like Twitter, Medium and LinkedIn have done a very good job of keeping readers on their sites, instead of linking out elsewhere. So I'd suggest publishing your posts at third-party sites (to reach readers where they are) and also at your own blog (as a record of your writing, and so visitors to your site can browse your thoughts).

Personally, I've become a huge fan of LinkedIn posts. (That's the shorter posts that appear in the feed, *not* the longer articles that you click off to.) At 1300 characters, they're just long enough to share a thought, a concept, an idea or a brief anecdote without getting bogged down in detail. They also get great engagement, and you can even attach images, movies or PDFs. Sometimes, I'll publish a concise post on LinkedIn, and a longer version on my own blog.

In sharing your thoughts, you'll have to decide how controversial you want to be. Rants, snark and takedowns tend to get more exposure, just because of the nature of social media, which favours extremes. However, they also draw more critical responses and even insults – which, for an introvert, can cut deep, particularly early on. These days, I think long and hard before I post anything too spicy, and try to remember the wise words of Benjamin Franklin: 'Whatever is begun in anger ends in shame.'

Takeaways from this chapter

- You may not like marketing, but you need it. It's how you generate future cash flow.

- Build your ideal marketing mix by choosing effective activities that you enjoy and can do consistently.

- Write a personal pitch and decide how you'll position yourself in the market.

- Get your website right – it's the single most important part of your marketing.

- Share your work and thoughts to build profile and credibility – and learn in the process.

7 SETTING AND AGREEING **PRICES**

Pricing is tough for all freelancers, but can be particularly so for introverts. In this chapter, we'll look at how to set your prices and present them to clients.

The problem with pricing

Pricing can be rough on the freelance introvert.

Setting a price means placing an objective value on your own work, putting it out there and imposing your will on the world. None of that comes easy if you're naturally reticent or self-effacing.

What's more, you might feel anxious that submitting a higher price will lead to some tricky conversations, in which you might be questioned, criticized or even rejected. And that could affect how you see your own value or ability.

Basically, pricing can take you into rocky emotional terrain. So you might look for ways to skirt around it.

One way is to stick with your existing clients, instead of seeking new ones. After all, if you're not pushing forward, no-one can knock you back. The problem is that it's far easier to quote higher for a new client than it is to jack up the rate for an existing one. So sticking with the same clients is a recipe for stagnant earnings, as well as the danger of 'too many eggs in one basket' if you only work for a handful of people.

Even if you do find new clients, you might still scale back your ambitions and set an 'introvert price' that isn't going to ruffle any feathers. Again, that means your earnings will flatline – or even go downhill.

Finally, you might simply spend too long thinking about your price, or procrastinate over submitting it. That doesn't cost you any money, unless you wait so long that you miss out on the job. But it does waste time – which, as we saw in chapter 4, is your most precious resource.

All this turns a new enquiry – which should be a happy event – into a trauma. Instead of making great strides forward, you get bogged down in uncertainty and self-doubt, putting up barriers to your own success. In this chapter, I'll share some ways to break through them.

How much will you charge?

Your prices will depend on a number of factors, including:

- **Your skills**: what you can do for clients, and how you add value for them

- **Your experience**: who you've worked for, doing which tasks and for how long

- **Your brand and reputation** – which really means the preconceptions (if any) that the client brings to their relationship with you (as we saw in chapter 6)

- The nature of the **market** for the service you offer

- The **'going rate'**, or what people tend to charge (although this is very much a movable feast)

- The **benefits** of the service you offer: how your work helps your clients' business

- General **perceptions** of those benefits – for example, is this a service that 'everybody needs', or more of a niche offering?

- The **industry** you serve, including how much money firms have to spend (for example, lawyers are probably richer than barbers)

- **Your location**, which can affect your cost of living and people's perceptions of costs

- **Your prospect's size and maturity**, which might affect their resources and cash flow (for example, startups may be poorer)

- **Your prospect's location**, which might affect their sensitivity to price (for example, firms in major cities may be accustomed to paying more).

As you can see, there are plenty of ingredients to go into the pot. But even if you could somehow get a computer to analyze all these factors, you still wouldn't be able to work out the one correct price to charge.

Even freelancers who seem very similar on paper can charge wildly different prices. Why is that?

The clue is in the softer elements of the list above – things like 'perceptions' and 'sensitivity'. You can't do anything about the experience you have, or the nature of your prospect's business. But what you *can* control is where you set your prices and how you present them to prospects. And that, in turn, depends on your own mindset and approach. So that's what the rest of this chapter is about.

Enter the deal zone

Freelancing is the Wild West of work. There are few rules and regulations, no fixed scales of charges, no higher authority you can refer to. Outside of a few online platforms, it's hard to find out what different freelancers charge, so you can compare their prices. Basically, it's just you and the prospect, trying to reach a deal.

That might sound daunting, but it's liberating too. Your prices are fluid and dynamic, continually being recreated in the here-and-now. You don't have to charge what others charge, or even what *you* charged up till now. Every new project is a chance to change. So while your earnings may be uncertain, they're also unconstrained.

It's a bit like buying a house. Yes, there's a vague range of acceptable prices, loosely based on the physical characteristics of the property. But the only 'right' or 'fair' price is the one that buyer and seller agree.

As a freelancer, you have a range of acceptable fees for a given project, from rock-bottom up to ideal. The prospect has their own range too, ranging from bargain up to tolerable. Where the two ranges overlap, you have a 'deal zone' of mutually acceptable prices. Your goal is to get as near to the top of that zone as you can.

How big is the deal zone? Probably bigger than you think. It may not always seem that way, because most of your freelance jobs will quickly home in on 'the price', which then feels solid and fixed to you. In reality, there might have been more money on the table than you thought.

You can't see the deal zone, and it varies from client to client. However, over time, feedback will hint at where the limits are. If nobody takes up your quotes, you're way out of bounds and need to rethink. If every quote turns into business, you're closer to the middle or lower end of the zone, so you might want to push upwards. And if you get *most* jobs, but not all, you're around the top – in the area where prospects think carefully about buying, but generally still buy.

That's the sweet spot, because it lets you balance your workload and your earnings. You'll get enough work, and earn good money from doing it. But because you won't take every job that comes your way, you'll have plenty of time to deliver quality work while avoiding stress and exhaustion.

How will you charge?

There are three main ways to price freelance projects: by time, by quantity and by project.

Charging by time means you set an hourly or daily rate and simply charge the client for the time you spend on the project.

It's simple and transparent, but it depends on your powers of prediction. Either you work out how long the job will take in advance, or you agree something more flexible where you give a rough estimate, track your hours and invoice for whatever you do.

Problems can arise if the prospect disputes your time estimate – or, indeed, your actual recorded hours – and you then get caught up in horse-trading over how long a job 'should' take. Or – even worse – you end up haggling over 'how much you could do in four hours'. That's a complete dead-end, and very far from being rewarded for the value you deliver.

However, a deeper problem with time charging is that it focuses on *inputs* rather than *outputs*. In other words, you're charging for the time you put in, rather than the value the client gets out. And there's little consideration of what you actually *do* in that time, or the extra value you add. You're like a chef who charges for the ingredients rather than the finished dish.

Time charging also penalizes the freelancer who is both a quick worker, and honest about it. As you move through your freelance career, you'll find that you learn how to do some tasks both better *and* faster.

Clients should still pay a premium for the quality that comes from your experience, however long the work actually takes you.

However, time charging does have its place. For example, if a client wants me to attend a meeting or an event, I say I'll charge on the basis of the time it takes me, usually with a minimum charge of half a day. If you do this, be realistic. If travelling to a two-hour meeting will prevent you from doing any other work that day, you should be charging the client for the full day. You may have to practise being assertive about this.

Charging by quantity means charging for each unit of something that you produce. It doesn't work for everyone, but writers (for example) can use per-word pricing for some projects. The problem is that not all words are equal – a three-word tagline might take as long to produce as a 3000-word article. (For example, I'm pretty sure Nike's 'Just do it' took way longer.) So again, quantity prices aren't usually the best way to reflect the value you deliver.

Finally, we have the best approach, in my opinion: **charging by the project**. With this method, you set out everything you will do on the project, and quote a single figure that covers it all. You'll certainly consider how long it will take, but just as important is the value the prospect will get from your work.

For example, suppose you're designing a website for a management consultant. It will be their shop window and first point of contact with nearly every client. They'll be using it to pull in mega-fee-paying business. So your price should reflect the *value* that it brings them – not just the number of hours you spend, or the size of the site in pages.

To reach a project price, it can be worth having a nominal daily rate to use as a rough basis. You can arrive at this by dividing your target earnings by the number of days you'll work. For example, £50,000 per annum divided by 240 working days (allowing for weekends and some holidays) = around £208 per day. So if you think a job might take you half a day, you might go for a price of £150, to allow for some contingencies. (You then quote this as a flat project price – you don't describe it as 'half a day'.)

Project pricing is a model of simplicity: one job, one price. It's also transparent, in the sense that you say exactly what you'll do, and deliver, for the money. It isn't transparent in terms of the time you put in – but that's your business, not the prospect's.

The only drawback of project pricing is that you have to consider the project carefully before you can price it – and the prospect has to give you the info you need in order to do that. Inevitably, that all takes time. On the upside, you get a chance to warm up the prospect by showcasing your knowledge and diligence during the quoting process. For example, you may be able to describe the approach you intend to take, without giving away too much about what you'll actually do.

Overall, you should choose the pricing method that gives you the most scope to set prices in a creative, flexible way. If the way you set prices is allowing you to develop your business and move towards your earnings target, that's great. But if it's holding you back, you need to think again.

Creating bundles

One way to save time on the pricing process is to turn particular batches of work into products, packages or bundles available at a fixed price. For example, a designer could produce a 'startup business pack' comprising a logo, a business card and a basic leaflet. You can make the price sound attractive by giving a nominal price for each element individually, then quoting a discounted price for all of them together.

Packages are easy to promote as being a good deal, and they have a solid, non-negotiable feel that makes prospects less likely to question them. And as long as you set the price wisely, you know you'll always be getting a good rate for the work.

Preset packages are also good for introverts, because they greatly reduce the interaction involved in quoting for jobs. You just put them up on your website and people can take them or leave them. On the downside, you may miss out on the opportunity to engage during the quoting process, as I mentioned above.

Frame your price

Imagine we're having a drink together. Just two introvert freelancers hanging out, talking pricing strategies. Suddenly, I pipe up, 'Hey, wanna buy my car? It's £5000.'

No matter how many beers you've sunk, you're going to ask a few questions before you give me an answer – even if you are in the market for a vehicle. And in the same way, you have to give your price some context so the prospect can understand what that number really means. The larger the project, the more important this becomes.

Before you say anything else to a prospect, *always* say 'Thank you for your enquiry. I would be very pleased to work on this project,' or something similar. That tells the prospect that their business is important to you, and acknowledges that they always have a choice of provider. You should say this even to your oldest, most familiar clients when they ask about a new project. It positions your proposal as a sincere desire to help, not just a business deal or a financial transaction.

For larger projects, go on to show why the prospect should choose you. If you feel that you're well suited to the project, say so. Point to previous work you've done, and say how it's relevant. If you can, mention results that you've achieved for other clients. If you've written any case studies (see chapter 6) you could link to them.

Now, briefly set out your proposal. Remember that projects involve a lot more than just the hands-on work.

Tasks that you might think of as optional extras, or 'just' preparation, are actually a central part of the value you offer.

For example, your quotes could include...

- Writing a detailed proposal or supporting notes for your work

- Attending meetings or talking to different people involved in the project

- Researching products, markets, competitors or customers

- Managing the project

- Developing ideas (that is, thinking as well as doing)

- Responding to feedback and making changes

- ...and so on.

Don't be afraid to include activities that are 'just thinking'. Remember, clients are hiring your *mind* – not just a pair of hands.

To give your price the right framing, mention it last. Say why you're right for the job, how you'll approach it and perhaps a timescale for delivery. Then, towards the end, say something like 'My price to carry out the work on this basis is £1250.' That will guide the prospect to think 'OK, so I get all these things, and that will cost me £1250.' If you say the price first, they'll immediately think, 'Really? So what do I get for that?', leaving the rest of your email playing a defensive game of catch-up.

The time and space to get it right

If your prospect doesn't like your proposal, they can just move on to someone else. But you have just one shot to close this deal. So when you're preparing a price for a significant project, give yourself plenty of time and space to get it right – particularly if you really want the work or the client.

Actually, your client needs time and space too, to make the right buying decision. If you're shooting for the top of the deal zone – like you should – they'll probably need a while to reflect on your price and decide to go ahead. They may also want to get some other proposals, and compare them with each other.

The worst way to discuss important prices, particularly for an introvert, is 'live', in real time. If a client asks you for a price when you're face to face, or on the phone, pretty much *any* reply you make will be hasty and ill-considered. What's more, you simply won't have the space to frame your price properly, as described above. As a result, you'll almost certainly quote too low – and regret it the very second the words leave your mouth.

Basically, you want to get the discussion into writing as soon as you can. If a client puts you on the spot, say something like, 'Can I give that some thought and send you an email later today?' They can hardly say no, and you can then take your time to put together a detailed, fully costed proposal.

This also applies to 'ballpark' prices. Prospects sometimes ask for these so they can make a quick like-for-like comparison between providers on the basis of price. That's understandable – but you want to shift the conversation to the *unique* value you offer on each project.

One way to deal with the 'ballpark' question is to reveal your nominal daily rate, as a basis for comparison with others. However, it's still just a number that means very little out of context. Whenever you can, make sure your prices include *words* as well as numbers. You should only throw out an unadorned ballpark price if you're not that bothered about getting the job.

Even ballpark prices can be framed a little. For example, when I quote my daily rate, I mention to the prospect that it puts me around the middle of the market. I'm not a creative hotshot who's written for the biggest brands, but I *have* been going for a while and helped a wide range of clients – as my testimonials show. Saying this encourages the prospect to reflect on whether I'd be right for them too.

The courage to click 'send'

Often, the biggest hurdle when pricing is when you finally fire off your quote. With that one click, you commit to your price, for better or worse. You're in the lap of the gods. For an introvert who likes to be in control, it's pretty daunting.

Let me tell you how I get over this obstacle. Maybe it will work for you too.

First, you arrive at a price that you're happy with, using whatever method works for you. But then, inside your mind, you consciously let go of all thoughts about the time you'll put in, how much you want the work, what other people charge, how much you've made this month, the bike you're dreaming of buying and so on. You also make a conscious decision to stop second-guessing the client's thoughts, or where the deal zone might be.

Those were the ingredients, but now the loaf is baked. Your price is *done*. And it can't be undone, any more than a loaf can be unbaked.

Your price then becomes nothing but a number written in an email. It's just an item of data being exchanged between two firms. In fact, it's not even 'your price' any more. It's *the* price. It's not 'what you charge'; it's simply what this project costs.

Actually, this mindset probably puts you closer to your prospect than you think. Yes, some clients are obsessively price-focused, and a few make everything personal (as we saw in chapter 5). But most are simply checking out a price.

Sure, they might notice that some prices are higher than others. But that's the nature of a market. Most probably, they'll just assume that a higher price denotes higher quality, greater skill or more experience. They're certainly not thinking ill of you as a person, just because you quoted a particular price for some work.

With that in mind, stop second-guessing the prospect, put the price back up to where you had it before and click 'send'. Whatever happens, you will be OK.

Putting prices on your website

This is quite a hot topic among freelancers, with some strongly in favour and others dead against.

The main reason for quoting prices on your website is transparency. Prospects can see instantly where you fall within the market, and what they can expect to pay. That can help to discourage timewasters and those who can't really afford you.

More subtly, you give an *impression* of being forthright and open, simply by giving your prices up front. And that might give prospects a positive vibe – regardless of how much you actually charge.

The downside is that you may not get to frame your price by linking it to the prospect's own project. They might arrive at your site, click on 'Prices', think 'Wow, that's a lot' and leave, without appreciating what they get for their money. And where some people see honesty, others might see boasting, or even arrogance. (However, national culture plays a big part here; in my experience, US freelancers are far more comfortable talking money than their UK counterparts. And elsewhere, things may be different again.)

Whatever you decide, you have to feel comfortable with it. Personally, I prefer to have some control over how and when money enters the conversation. But I do know that many freelancers publicize their prices, and they seem perfectly happy with the results.

As an introvert, you might like the idea of your website doing the talking for you, selling your services and weeding out the timewasters on your behalf.
But equally, you might feel a little over-exposed, telling the world how much you earn. At the end of the day, it's your call.

Giving discounts

Sooner or later, everybody comes across a prospect who plays hardball on price. If you're struggling for work, this situation can be really stressful. Nevertheless, you must find a way to deal with it without completely caving in.

Prospects may give a range of reasons for wanting a discount. Some people just try for one on principle, or as a company-wide policy of cost control. But as we saw in chapter 5, a request for a discount can also be an attempt to gain the upper hand at the start of a relationship.

If you feel uncomfortable about a request for a discount, or the way it's made, the time to act on your intuition is now, by politely but firmly declining the project. Some prospects will then back down and try to play nice – but in a way, the damage is already done. Whether you keep talking is up to you.

Some prospects will point out that they're a small business or a startup, and money is therefore tight. The obvious retort is that you are *also* a small business – and not a charity. However, startups *can* be a special case. Getting in early as their 'go-to guy' could be good for you if the business survives and thrives. You could also play a big part in their development, or get a chance to work on things that might otherwise be out of reach, like helping to build a brand from scratch.

If you're happy to offer a discount in principle, try not to undercut yourself. First, ask the client what they'd be willing to pay. This is perfectly reasonable, since you've put forward your price first. If they propose a price, you can decide whether to accept it or make a counter-proposal. If they refuse to say, offer a nominal discount like 10% and see where that takes you.

The client might have a fixed budget, and ask you to work within it. If it falls outside your deal zone, you could offer to reduce the scope (in other words, just do part of the project) rather than agree to do everything for the reduced price. That way, you get to go ahead and work with the client, but without giving any ground on price. The client also gets to save face, since their precious budget is intact. And they might like your work so much that they ask you to do the rest of the project anyway. When push comes to shove, and the client knows you can deliver, many budgets are a *lot* stretchier than they first appear.

Working for free

Why would you ever want to work for free? Well, in your early days, you might want to build up your skills or experience. You might want to generate projects for your portfolio, or positive testimonials (see chapter 6). You might feel that doing free work will help you gain a particular client – or provide a stepping stone to other, more lucrative clients later on.

Apart from these self-interested reasons, you might want to help a friend, family member or good cause. If so, you can get all the benefits above, plus the satisfaction of making a difference. Many well-established freelancers do *pro bono* work for this reason alone.

The main problem with free work is obvious: no money. But beyond that, it can also skew your relationship with the client. On your side, you may end up feeling resentful or put upon. And on their side, they may not take the project completely seriously, or respect its boundaries, because they have no financial 'skin in the game'.

To guard against this, make sure you agree exactly what you're offering to do, so there's no misunderstanding later on. You may also want to consider how much experience your client has of commissioning freelance work, and what that might mean for you. Sometimes, working for a friend is actually trickier than working for a stranger, simply because they have no idea how the relationship should work, and it's embarrassing if you have to lay down the law. No work experience is worth falling out with a friend.

Doing free samples

Sometimes, prospects will ask you to do a free sample before the project begins. They might say something like, 'We need to see what you can do for us before we commit.'

The rationale for this is that even though you may already have a portfolio they can look at, the prospect wants to know what you can do for them *specifically*. I'll let you decide whether that's a valid argument or not.

If there isn't much time commitment, and you're not too busy with other things, knocking off a free sample *could* be OK. But you still need to go in with your eyes open.

The first issue is the nature of the arrangement. Who else is involved? Who are you being compared with, and how? What's the basis for comparison or evaluation? Are you guaranteed any work if you pass the test, or is the prospect just testing the market? (I've even had an approach where someone had clearly parcelled out a big editing job into sections, and sent each one to a different freelancer as a 'sample' to try and get the whole job done for free!)

The second problem is putting the cart before the horse. Most freelancers need to spend time getting to know the client and the project before they can do their best work, or even submit a proper proposal. You may show willing by jumping right in at the deep end, but if you sink rather than swim, you haven't really helped anyone.

By the same token, you're unlikely to do your best work if you're constantly worrying about how much time you're spending on this thing. Whether it's no fee or just a low fee, being paid less than you're worth is the most powerful demotivator there is.

One response to a request for a free sample is to offer a paid one instead. For instance, you say you'll do part of the project and submit it to the client. If they like it, you'll continue. If they don't, you'll invoice an agreed amount, and walk away with no hard feelings.

However, this approach only works if the project can actually be split up. As a copywriter, I can sometimes write (for example) one or two pages of a website, and get them to a reasonably finished state. However, if the project requires a lot of research, that might not work so well. And for some disciplines, it might not work at all. For example, a logo designer would either have to show preliminary sketches (which aren't representative of finished work) or a near-final design that the client could just take and use.

When you don't get paid

Sooner or later, every freelancer has to deal with not being paid. It's rare, and you need to keep it in proportion – for example, my own bad debts represent less than 0.5% of my total earnings since I started freelancing. But it can happen.

You can minimize the problem with a contract (as we saw in chapter 3). But whatever you have in writing, clients can still not pay. You then embark on a process of trying to call them, sending ever-more strongly worded letters and perhaps taking legal action. If your client is overseas, this whole process is far more complex, and can quickly become more trouble than it's worth (as your unscrupulous client well knows).

Not all debts are equal. You need to weigh the value of the invoice against the opportunity cost of pursuing it. For example, if your unpaid debt is for two days' work and you might end up spending a day chasing it, the net result will be one day's pay. You could just as easily forget the debt, work a day for another client and get the same financial outcome – plus a far sunnier mood and a sense of progress.

Of course, you've still lost those two days from before, but that is what economists call a 'sunk cost'. Your time is used up and gone no matter what you do. What really matters is the choice you make now.

For me, the biggest factor is the emotional labour that pursuing a debt demands. I've chased plenty of non-payers in the past, and even taken one to court. I found that the constant weight of resentment, anger and paranoia took a toll that ultimately outweighed the money itself. And if I never got the money anyway, that just made it worse. So if you're secretly longing to write off a debt just to be rid of the emotional baggage, give yourself a break and let it go.

The five stages of freelance pricing

I've found that I've moved through different attitudes to pricing over the years – usually forwards, but sometimes taking a step back too. I call these the five stages of freelance pricing.

At **Stage 1**, you think, 'They'll choose me if I'm cheaper.' When you're starting out, an entry-level price feels right. You're not that confident yet, plus you're an introvert – so it's reassuring not to expose yourself too much.

Being cheaper can take the form of simply pitching a low price overall, or other approaches that amount to the same thing, such as introductory or bulk discounts, free samples, taking on additional tasks without charging extra and so on.

The problem with going in low is that you reap what you sow. If your prices are based in insecurity or caution, you project those feelings into the market, where prospects pick up on them and reflect them. Cheapness begets cheapness.

Here's the thing: price affects how people perceive value. Think about your weekly supermarket shop. Do you see cheaper products as better quality, or worse? By trying to lure in a prospect with a low price, you could actually be pushing them away – or just making your competitors look better by comparison.

At **Stage 2**, you start believing that you are a viable provider, just like everyone else. And that makes you ask, 'What does everyone else charge?' So you start looking out at the market – something that, as an introvert, you might have been less willing to do until now.

You can get some idea from 'find a freelancer' sites like Upwork, Odesk, Fiverr and Elance – although the prices you see there are likely to be on the low side. You might also find useful benchmarks from trade organizations or earnings surveys. Or you could befriend a fellow freelancer and ask them what they charge.

When you price at the market rate, you can cite something to back up your prices. That feels good if you're naturally modest. The downside is that you can't increase your prices above that going rate without abandoning the third-party support.

At **Stage 3**, you think, 'I've been doing this a while now.' It dawns on you that the rates you've heard about are not handed down from on high, engraved on stone tablets. They're constantly shifting as freelancers out there in the market agree prices with real-world clients. You are not powerless.

Plus you now have some experience under your belt. You've probably gained some repeat clients, and received some word-of mouth referrals. If you stay on the same track, your business is likely to keep growing. That gives you the security and confidence to base your prices on your own skills and experience, rather than defining yourself in relation to others.

You're an introvert, so it might feel scary to just strike out and set your own rate. If so, try adding 25% to the going rate, or something similar. You're still in touch with the market – you're just edging towards the top end of it.

By this point, you've been through the mill and you're still standing. You've gained clients, held on to clients, lost clients. You've missed out on some jobs, messed up others. But above all, you've done a lot of solid, high-quality work that has delivered real value for clients. You've arrived at **Stage 4**, when you ask, 'What's it really worth?'

Now, if someone asks you for (say) a new logo design, you don't ask yourself what others charge, or how long it might take, or even what you've charged before. You ask yourself *what it's worth to the client*. And if they're going to use it on everything they produce for the next 10 years, the price should reflect that.

Finally, at **Stage 5**, you simply say, 'If you want me, that's what it costs.' You quote the rate at which you will be 100% happy to do the job, regardless of your current workload and the way the job pans out. There's no second-guessing or self-sabotage. You don't even think that much about whether or not you will get the job. But at the same time, your price is not extortionate, or completely detached from the market.

You'll probably take several years of hard graft to reach this point. It's the stage at which you are, finally, secure – psychologically, professionally and financially.

If you get to be very high-profile, so your reputation precedes you, Stage 5 will be your natural home. However, you might also end up here purely due to supply and demand. In other words, referrals and repeat business fill up your calendar to the point where you have to turn stuff down. (I usually feel that I'm around Stage 4, tipping into Stage 5 when I'm really busy.)

Takeaways from this chapter

- Pricing can be tough, but it's important to get it right.

- Set prices to reflect the value you offer, and aim for the top of the deal zone.

- Choose the pricing method that works for you and helps you move forward.

- Take time to prepare your prices and frame them in the right way.

- Only offer discounts, free work or free samples when the deal is right for you.

- Check your progress through the five stages of freelance pricing, and think about how you could move on to the next stage.

8 BUILDING YOUR **CONFIDENCE**

Confidence doesn't always come easy to freelance introverts, but you have to believe in your skills in order to market them. This chapter looks at ways to build your self-belief.

Why confidence matters

Going freelance isn't just a new way of working. It's a new way of living. Your work, your money, your leisure time, your home life, your family and even your health are all interlinked, and affected by each and every choice you make. Your timetable is constantly shifting, as are clients' demands. You have to hustle for every penny, and there's no rule that says your work must add up to a neat eight-hour day or five-day week.

It's a reality that nobody in a regular job can ever truly understand. And it's a tough place to build up your confidence.

It would be OK if confidence was just a superficial thing. But it's not. Your confidence touches every aspect of your work, because you can only use your skills to the extent that you believe in them. And if you don't believe you can do something, you won't even try to do it. As Henry Ford said, 'Whether you believe you can, or believe you can't, you're right.'

All this is even more important for introverts, who tend to be modest and self-deprecating. Even if you feel sure of your ability inside your head, you may still feel reticent about projecting that into the world. And because you listen so carefully to what people say, you may also take criticism – or just perceived criticism – to heart, allowing one or two pieces of negative feedback to overwhelm all the good things people have said about you.

Although this chapter is about building up your confidence, it's not about forcing yourself to be an extrovert. In fact, it's much more about your *inner* life: how you talk to yourself, and how you feel about your own skills and character. Growing in confidence will give you more choices – but you're still free to make those choices in line with the way you are.

Building confidence step by step

If confidence affects ability, it follows that you should actively work on it, not just passively accept it as 'how you are'. Just as you develop your hands-on skills, so you should develop your confidence in those skills. That's what makes the difference between a hobby and a viable freelance career.

The first step to becoming confident is deciding to be confident. I'm not saying that you'll magically become confident as soon as you make that decision – just that you won't *start* becoming confident until you do. The choice to be confident is necessary, but not sufficient. If you want to climb the top step, you have to climb the bottom ones first.

Perhaps there will be many steps to climb before you feel truly confident. But none of them will happen unless you want them to. You're not going to 'just' become confident, any more than you're going to 'just' learn Chinese. And you're certainly not going to become confident against your will.

Once you've made that choice, you can build confidence by edging outside your comfort zone whenever you get the opportunity to do so. The best opportunity is when a longstanding client asks you to do something you've never done before, because you're already their 'go-to guy' for other things. They're already well disposed towards you, so you don't have to worry so much about messing it up.

Beyond your comfort zone

In 2013, I hosted the first ProCopywriters conference in London. As co-founder of the organization, I had to address an audience of around 200 people, welcoming delegates in the morning and introducing speakers throughout the day.

An extrovert would have handled it with ease – probably even enjoyed it. For me, it was an absolute nightmare. The 'reachback' from the event extended over months, casting a shadow over my whole summer. I practised my lines, visualized success, learnt how to breathe and stay calm. But I still felt a cold shiver of dread every time I remembered what was coming. Even though I confessed my nerves to the other organizers, I don't think they had the faintest idea what I was really going through.

In the end it was fine. I was pretty wooden, but I got through it. There was plenty of goodwill in the room; people wanted me to do well. And even if they hadn't, what's the worst that could happen?

Nevertheless, I promised myself I'd never speak in public again. I had been there and done it, but I had no desire to go back.

Later on, we gathered feedback forms about the event. They vividly illustrated the principle that you can't please all the people all of the time. Taken as a whole, the feedback was overwhelmingly positive – certainly as good as we could hope for, given the diverse profiles of the delegates who came along. But what did I carry around in my head for days? That's right – the handful of negative comments.

Going outside your comfort zone is supposed to help you grow, whether personally or professionally. We're taught that these highly challenging experiences are part of business success.

The problem is, an experience that might be merely uncomfortable for an extrovert can be utterly terrifying for an introvert, to the point where the pain outweighs the gain. When you take everything into account, putting yourself through things like that just doesn't do you any good.

So, when you're considering this sort of opportunity, you need to carry out a sort of personal cost/benefit analysis. Consider how far you're venturing outside your comfort zone, and in what direction. Be honest about what it will give you – and what it will take away.

Ask yourself:

- Why do I want to do this activity or project?

- How will it help me? Am I doing it to gain something specific, or just to stretch myself?

- How different and challenging will it be? Realistically, how difficult am I going to find it?

- Is there a chance that I'll receive negative feedback about it? If so, how will I deal with that?

- Is it something I want to start doing regularly, or just a one-off?

As you can see, some activities are one-time-only experiences that you do to prove something to yourself, while others are about gaining skills you could use regularly over time. Either can be worthwhile, but it's important to be clear on the difference, so you know how much time and effort to invest.

Actually, you might find that you like it outside your comfort zone. When I finished my first book, *Copywriting Made Simple*,[10] I promised myself I'd never do anything so arduous again. A few months later, I began work on this one.

Your explanatory style

Back when I was working nine to five, I once told my boss that I wasn't enjoying my work, and was thinking about going freelance. But he dismissed my concerns by saying that if I did, I'd very soon be 'scrabbling around for work'.

His words really hit home. They convinced me that I wasn't cut out for freelancing somehow, or that freelancing itself just wasn't viable as a lifestyle. And because I took that to heart, it was many years before I tried freelancing for myself.

However, there's another way to look at this story. My boss wasn't really predicting my freelancing experience; he was recalling his own. What's more, he clearly had an agenda: he didn't want his valuable team member – who he'd just spent months training up – to walk out the door. Basically, he was talking about himself, not me.

---

[10] Learn more at https://www.copywritingmadesimple.info

When things like this happen, different people react in different ways. Some internalize the causes of events, while others see those causes as outside themselves. And what makes the difference is their *explanatory style*.

If your personal explanatory style is optimistic, you tend to blame others for negative events and take credit for good ones. You also assume that negative situations will be temporary, and that they only relate to certain specific things.

If you have a pessimistic explanatory style, it's the other way round. You often blame bad events on yourself, and give all the credit for good ones to other people. You tend to think that negative situations will be around for ever, and that they'll affect everything.

Extroverts tend to have an optimistic explanatory style for positive outcomes, while introverts tend to have a pessimistic style for negative ones.[11] Because we introverts often turn inwards to brood and ponder, we tend to blame ourselves when things go wrong – even when they're not really our fault. Very pessimistic explanatory styles have also been linked with depression.[12]

---

[11] Cheng, H. and Furnham, A. 'Attributional Style and Personality as Predictors of Happiness and Mental Health', *Journal of Happiness Studies* 2, 307–327 (2001)

[12] Sanjuán, P. and Magallares, A., 'A longitudinal study of the negative explanatory style and attributions of uncontrollability as predictors of depressive symptoms,' *Personality and Individual Differences*, 46 (2009), 714–718

Once you're aware of your explanatory style, you can consciously aim to change it. While you can't control what happens to you, you *can* control how you think about it – and that in turn affects how you respond to it. Some responses close down your options and reduce your control, while others give you power, perspective and choice.

In my story, the words my boss actually spoke were 'Go freelance and you'll struggle for work.'
My pessimistic explanation of that was 'He's talking about me. I could never be a freelancer'. But instead, I could have chosen a optimistic explanation: something like, 'He's talking about his own life, not mine. My experience will be different from that.'

This table shows a few things you might hear from your clients, and how you could interpret them in different ways.

What the client says	Pessimistic explanation	Optimistic explanation
'Can you offer us a lower price?'	'They'll only use me if I reduce the price'	'They obviously want to use me, so I don't have to reduce the price'
'We're not sure about the direction you've taken'	'I'm incompetent. I'll never get this right'	'The brief wasn't clear and detailed enough. I just need more information'

'We'd like you to make a few changes'	'They don't like my work'	'They like most of what I've done. I'm nearly there'
'We really like your work'	'They're only saying that because they don't really know what they're talking about'	'They're saying that because I am talented and professional'

The same applies to situations you might come across as a freelancer. For example, suppose you discover that there are lots of local freelancers working in the same area as you. You might think, 'There's too many of us. There'll never be enough work to go round.' But you could just as easily think, 'There must be a lot of work in the local area, to support all these freelancers.'

Or you might look at another, well-established freelancer's website and feel in awe of their experience, testimonials or clients. The pessimistic view would be 'That's so depressing. I'll never be like them.' But the optimistic angle is 'Wow, amazing! If I keep going, that's where I'll be one day.'

Remember, this isn't about working out what's 'really' going on. It's about how you *interpret* real-world events. And some interpretations are more helpful than others.

Impostor syndrome

Impostor syndrome is the feeling that you can't really do the work you've been asked to do, and that you're going to get 'found out' somehow.

Impostor syndrome has no relation to actual ability. Even very experienced professionals, with hugely impressive achievements, get it from time to time.

I get it too. Even after well over a decade as a freelance writer, I'm still tormented by doubts before I start some jobs. *I won't understand the topic. I won't be able to meet the brief. I won't have any ideas.*

One way I get over that feeling is to picture the actual hands-on tasks that I will soon be doing: reading through the source material, creating a document, setting up headings. In my mind, this turns the job into a safe, predictable process that I just have to move through step by step, as opposed to a voyage into the unknown. I've made that journey before, so I can do it again.

Once I get to the hands-on stage, I find it really helpful to *just start*. It really doesn't matter what I do, as long as I do *something*. I write the ending first. I write a weak headline, a silly joke, a wordy description. I write my thoughts about the project itself, and how I don't think I can do it. I know none of this can actually be used. But once I get into improving what's there, instead of creating from scratch, everything seems easier.

Another way to tackle impostor syndrome is to watch yourself at work. Next time you're working on a project you enjoy, use part of your mind to observe your thoughts as they unfold. Reach into your unconscious processes, and bring them into conscious awareness. This sort of 'looking inwards' comes easy to introverts.

For example, you could notice…

- How you make the right choices about the elements of your work, whatever they are – colours and fonts, words and formats, materials and processes, templates and plugins, ingredients and recipes, plants and designs

- How you express your ideas, or encourage others to express theirs

- How you see straight away what's working well, and what needs to change

- How you choose your words, and put them in the right order

- How you question a brief, or suggest a better way

- How you think ahead, anticipating the effect of your decisions and how others might react

- How your thinking evolves over the project, and how you build this emerging insight into your work

- How you know which paths *not* to take, because your experience has shown you that they just lead to dead ends or wrong destinations.

By knowing what to do at every turning point, you guide a project forward and add value for your clients. These myriad micro-decisions are the foundations of your ability. Together, the little details form a big picture of someone who is professional, capable and talented – even if you can't always see that image yourself.

Finally, you can also refer back to your own testimonials (see chapter 6). You got them to persuade prospects – but you can also use them to persuade *yourself*. Remember what you did for the client, read their positive comments and believe what they say. Because it's true.

A word about social media

As we've seen, social media can be an important means of support when you're working on your own. However, it can also have a big impact on your confidence – and not always for the better.

Personally, I find social media makes a good mood better, but a bad one worse. If you're feeling upbeat, and you put that out into the world, you'll get more positivity in return. But if you're feeling sad, anxious or insecure, and you go online hoping for a pick-me-up, you may be disappointed.

The problem is that when you look at other people's content through a low mood, it's easy to lapse into 'compare and despair'. Sentiments that bring inspiration to others just bring desperation to you. If others are go-getting, you feel lazy. If others are sharing wonderful creative work, you feel dull and pedestrian. If others are being upbeat and engaged, you feel alienated.

The lesson is not to compare your lows with other people's highs. Remember that the version of themselves people put online is edited, partial and possibly straight-out fantasy. Their real life is what happens when they're *away* from the screen. And it's probably not so different from yours.

Sometimes, we treat social media like an emotional lottery, gambling time and attention in the hope of a big payoff. But there's no jackpot that will repay those wasted hours. The best you're going to get is the fleeting satisfaction of a few likes, a funny joke or a kind reply. So instead of endlessly scrolling, log off and do something more constructive. Something that will build up your confidence – or, at least, not undermine it.

If you find it hard to switch off, be more introvert! Don't think of social media as a solo pastime or a necessary work activity. Instead, think of it as a party you don't really want to go to, or a meeting you'd rather not attend. When you look at your feed and ask yourself, 'Do I really want to hear all these voices right now?' you'll often find the honest answer is 'no'.

Takeaways from this chapter

- Confidence is important because you can only use your abilities if you believe in them, and can project them into the world.

- To build your confidence step by step, gradually move outside your comfort zone, ideally with the support of your best clients.

- Understand your explanatory style so you can choose more optimistic interpretations of events.

- Beat impostor syndrome by getting back in touch with your own abilities.

- If social media is undermining your confidence, log off and do something that enhances it instead.

9 CHOOSING YOUR BELIEFS

Your beliefs determine your focus, which determines your success. So choose them wisely.

Why beliefs matter

Your beliefs are your window on the world. They determine what you focus on, what you think about and how you feel. That, in turn, can affect your goals, your decisions and your actions. In other words, your beliefs shape your reality, including your fortunes as a freelancer.

Beliefs don't always reflect the objective truth about the world. For example, different people have very different personal beliefs about things like politics and religion. As Anaïs Nin said, 'We don't see the world as it is; we see it as we are.'

We all know that life has its ups and downs. That's an objective fact. But while one person might experience that reality and conclude that *life is a struggle*, another might decide that *life is a game*. And their expectations will be very different as a result of what they believe.

It's easy to think of beliefs as a fixed aspect of your personality – like being an introvert. In fact, they're only formed by chance events, and they're always changing and evolving too. I'm sure you can remember a time when you experienced something new, and your beliefs changed as a result.

It follows that you can actively *choose* the beliefs you want to hold. You can think of them like different pairs of glasses that you put on when you need to see the world in different ways. You can choose the beliefs that support you and help you achieve your goals, and let go of those that hold you back.

Remember, this isn't about denying reality, or retreating into fantasy. You can choose one interpretation over another without living in cloud-cuckoo land. Beliefs are simply tools that you choose to get things done.

Overcome self-limiting beliefs

Most of this chapter is devoted to positive beliefs that will help you move forward. But first, let's consider the negative ones that might be holding you back.

A self-limiting belief is something you say about yourself or the world, and accept as true. It usually takes the form of an unchangeable circumstance or personal trait that stops you from doing something:

- 'I can't do X (because I don't have the right experience / I'm too old / I'm too young / I'm too introverted, etc).'

- 'I could never do X. I'm just not that type of person.'

- 'I always get things like X wrong.'

These beliefs are 'self-limiting' because they are limits that you impose on yourself, not external constraints. So you can choose to let them go and adopt a new belief instead.

You might have self-limiting beliefs about your introversion simply because of the way society is. You see so many successful extroverts that you start believing that's the only way to succeed.

To discover your self-limiting beliefs, listen to your own words. That includes the things you say to other people, and how you talk to yourself inside your head (or even, perhaps, out loud). Tune into the voice of your inner critic, and what it tells you. Then, when you notice a self-limiting belief, ask yourself:

- Is this really true?

- How do I know it's true?

- Have there been times when it *wasn't* true?

These questions challenge you to find evidence for and against the self-limiting belief. You'll usually find that there are only a few events (if any) to support it – and plenty more events that suggest the opposite. You can use that knowledge to create new, self-liberating beliefs. Here are three methods you can use.

The first is to switch the emphasis from *being* and *having* to *doing*. For example, if you think, 'I'm not a good public speaker,' that's about *being* a certain way. Or, if you think, 'I just don't have public-speaking skills,' that's about having (or lacking) a particular thing. The implication is that it's difficult to change the way you are, or to acquire this rare quality.

However, if you say 'I haven't done any public speaking,' things already look different. Now, you're just describing reality. OK, you haven't spoken in public before. But that doesn't mean you can't do it now, or in the future.

The second method is to switch from saying *can't* to *can*. For example, instead of saying (for example) 'I can't do public speaking because I get too nervous,' say 'I *can* speak in public because…' and find a new ending for the sentence. With this method, you simply replace the self-limiting belief with an empowering one.

Alternatively, instead of confronting the limitation head-on, look for ways around it. For example, instead of saying, 'I can't speak in public,' you could say 'I haven't spoken in public yet. But I have presented my work to clients, which is similar, just on a smaller scale.'

If you focus on what you can't do, you're arguing for your own limitations – making the case for things to stay the same. But if you focus on what you *can* do, you tap into the power you have to change your situation.

And there is *always* something you can do, even if it's just going online and researching your options. Each step you take will reveal the next one.

The third method is to switch from *permanence* to *progress*. That means dropping absolute words like 'always' and 'never', which rule out any possibility of change. Instead, refocus on things that you're doing, or could do, to make a change.

So instead of saying 'I could never speak in public,' you simply say 'I haven't spoken in public yet.' Again, that's just a neutral description of events, with no judgement about the future. OK, maybe you don't do a lot of public speaking right now. But you *could*.

In the same way, instead of saying 'I always mess it up when I speak in public,' say something like 'I'm still learning public speaking.' Now the focus is on how you're moving forward, rather than a fixed situation that you're powerless to change.

The rest of this chapter describes some positive beliefs that might be useful in your freelance life, particularly as an introvert. Remember, they're not necessarily true – just potentially useful. So pick them up when they help you, and put them down when they don't.

You can choose

This simple belief highlights that you have a choice, at every moment, to do things differently. No matter what has happened so far, the future doesn't have to be like the past. And if you aren't getting the result you want, you need to try something new.

You already have all the resources you need

This belief, which is a basic principle of NLP, puts you in a position of power. It says that you already have the capability to start changing your situation.

At this moment, you may not be prepared to tackle every imaginable type of project, or deal with any circumstance that arises. But you *do* have the ability to learn, gain skills and make preparations.

Let's say you're planning to travel to China. Obviously, it would be helpful to speak some Chinese – and right now, you don't. However, you know how to find a class or a tutor. You know where to get hold of a book or an app that can help. You can think of times during the week when you could practise. And you know, from past experience, that as you move along these paths, more and more paths will come into view.

In other words, you can see the stepping stones from where you are now to where you want to be. It's just a question of using the resources you already have to obtain new ones. You can accomplish any task if you break it down into smaller steps, and just make a start.

The value you offer is unique

Early on in your freelance career, you may sometimes feel like you're just getting away with it. Yes, you've done a few jobs for a few clients. But did you really help them that much? Couldn't somebody else have done a far better job? Even after many years' freelancing, you might still feel that other freelancers could do exactly the same thing – maybe cheaper.

It's easy to fall into impostor syndrome, which we saw in chapter 8 – the feeling that you're going to be found out. Or you might start thinking that your success is all down to good fortune – and your luck could easily run out any day.

This belief reminds you that clients work with you because *they want to*. They want the service that only you can provide. They have a choice, and they chose you.

Any other options they might have had are beside the point. They're like other dishes on the menu that your clients didn't order. However tasty they sounded, in the end they just didn't want them.

On a purely technical level, it's true that your service probably *isn't* one of a kind. But your relationship with a client, and the personality, approach and values you bring, are important parts of the deal – and they *are* unique. Once a client trusts you, and values that relationship, they'll want to stay loyal. And that's nothing to do with luck, and everything to do with the value you offer.

Success lies on the far side of failure

As Thomas Edison said, 'I haven't failed. I've just found 10,000 ways that won't work.' This belief helps you keep going if you don't find an answer straight away.

Sometimes, you have to work through some bad ideas before you reach the good ones. That means getting comfortable with making mistakes and learning from them. In fact, it means actively seeking out opportunities to experiment, even if they involve 'failure', because you know that's the route to success.

Maybe you're a 'fixer' or 'completer-finisher' like me – someone who likes getting things done and dusted as quickly as possible. That can be a positive trait for a freelancer, because it means you follow through diligently on client projects. However, it can also cause you some anxiety if the right answer takes a while to emerge.

This belief guards against the tendency to give up when things don't work out. It gives you the perspective that you're actually working through a process, not stuck at the starting line. If you spend enough time with this problem, you will surely find an answer.

Everything happens for a reason

Now, this one is a double-edged sword. On the positive side, it helps you find the positive angle on every situation. If something goes wrong, instead of throwing your hands up in the air, you sit down and think about what you need to learn, or what you need to change. That can help to pull you out of self-pity and get you back on the road.

However, you can take this belief too far. If you look too hard for the reasons behind everything, you can end up blaming everything on yourself, including things other people have done that were objectively wrong or hurtful. So don't go looking for the meaning in something painful if you're better off letting it go. (This links in to your explanatory style, which we saw in chapter 8.)

Every effort brings some reward

This is a more practical version of the previous belief. It says that you will *always* gain something valuable from *any* effort you make to improve your freelance life – even if it's only the knowledge that a particular approach doesn't work.

This belief protects you from the sense of failure, futility or wasted time. It reminds you that there is great power in just beginning something, even if you don't yet have all the answers. And even if you don't finish it, you will still learn something from the experience, or gain something you can use somewhere else. There's no failure, only feedback.

Things will keep getting better

This belief is about accepting that positive trends are more likely to continue as they have done in the past, rather than reverse on a dime. It can help you combat the irrational fear that everything is about to go south, or that you're suddenly going to lose everything.

For example, if you've steadily gained one or two clients a month since you started freelancing, the most likely future is for that to carry on happening. If your earnings have steadily grown, they're most likely to keep on growing. Basically, if you keep on doing what you've been doing, you'll tend to keep getting what you've been getting.

Obviously, disasters can happen. For example, I'm writing this during the coronavirus crisis, with an inbox that's almost empty. But that's an external force that I can't do anything about – it doesn't invalidate everything that's allowed me to succeed so far. So I'm using the time to write this book and wait for the work to return. And if it doesn't, well, I'll do something else.

Your position is secure

There's a lazy, clichéd view that freelancing is inherently insecure. People sometimes talk about 'living hand to mouth', as if every freelancer lives under the constant threat of starvation. If you take this belief to heart, you can feel constantly afraid that your career is a house of cards that might collapse at any moment.

There's an important distinction between *consistency* and *security*. Someone in a salaried role may have a consistent, regular income, but that doesn't necessarily mean it's secure. For example, they may be at the mercy of a boss who can turn against them at any time. Or the firm they work for might be struggling, and secretly deciding who they're going to lay off next.

On the flip side, your freelance income may fluctuate wildly from month to month, but when you take a step back, you see that it has evened out to a solid annual income for several years. Instead of one boss, or one employer, you have 10, 20 or even more clients, all of whom can bring you work. You have skills that have proven their value in the market, and been publicly recognized by your clients. And you have the ability to gain new clients and new skills, if your situation demands it.

This is a useful belief if you have a dry spell. Even after several years of success, having no work can make you feel pretty anxious. My advice is to use the time for a creative project or a job you've been putting off – because you'll be back to the grindstone before you know it.

Everything is in its right place

This is a Zen belief that can help when you're worrying that you have too much to do, or too far to go, or that things just aren't working out. You can get a sort of 'scattered' feeling, as if nothing is ever quite done or finished, and your freelance career will never come together the way you want.

If you're waiting to feel like you've 'arrived' as a freelancer, you could be waiting a long time. In truth, a freelance role never really feels 'done and dusted' in the same way as a salaried position is neatly wrapped up with a job title, a list of responsibilities and a reward package. You are always gaining and losing clients, developing your service, learning new things and evolving your beliefs. Your business, and the way you present it, never stands still.

In reality, that's a good thing. But if you start seeing it as a negative, you might end up with a constant, creeping sense of dissatisfaction and incompleteness. So if your clients are happy and your bills are paid this month, give yourself a break and call that success.

Hold on tightly, let go lightly

This is maybe more of a motto than a belief, but I still find it very valuable.

It captures the idea that freelancing is all about balance. There are times when you need to go all in, and times you need to walk away.

It means that...

- You put forward a strong proposal and a good price, but if you don't win the project, you forget about it.

- If you do win the project, you do it to the best of your ability, but once it's done, you move on to the next one.

- You serve your clients as well as you can, but if they move on, you accept it with good grace.

- You hold on to your beliefs for as long as they're useful, but let go of them if they're not.

Heraclitus said, 'No man ever steps in the same river twice, for it's not the same river and he's not the same man.' Freelancing is like that. Everything is always flowing onward, and few things stay the same – including yourself. Making it work is about knowing when to move on, and accepting that even the very best things must come to an end.

Letting go isn't always easy for introverts, who like to hold on to a few things they love dearly. But it's an important lesson to learn about freelance work, even if you don't necessarily carry it through into the rest of your life.

This too shall pass

This is one for when things aren't going so well.

There is such a thing as being *too* positive, to the point where it becomes a hindrance rather than a help. Some people call it 'toxic positivity'. You try so hard to be positive that you end up smothering other, equally important emotions that you also need to feel.

It's true that you probably need a certain amount of optimism just to get going as a freelancer. But at the same time, you are allowed to feel bad when things don't work out. Some experiences, like losing a valued client or making a mistake on a project you really wanted, are just plain bad. There's not much point in sugar-coating them.

Sometimes, a bad feeling can be a sign of something that needs to change – just as physical pain is a sign that something is wrong with your body. For example, your emotions can alert you to problems with setting boundaries (chapter 3) or rogue clients (chapter 5).

However, at other times, your negative emotion is a phase that you need to move through. You just have to sit with it until it naturally passes away.

Don't tell yourself that you shouldn't be feeling this way, or that it's your fault because of who you are, or how you are. It isn't. Freelancing has its own weather, and this is the rain. No matter how bad things seem today, they will look different tomorrow. You'll find out new things, meet new people, have new ideas. Even if you have to make a really radical change in order to make progress, you *will* move on. This too shall pass.

Takeaways from this chapter

- Your beliefs are your window on the world. You can choose to adopt helpful beliefs.

10 OVER TO **YOU**

Thanks for reading this far.

We've looked at how to plan your freelance career, set up your business and set goals. We've looked at how to manage your time, set prices and work with clients. And we've explored ways to build your confidence and choose helpful beliefs.

Along the way, I've aimed to share some of the lessons from my freelance life. I hope you find them useful.

However, do bear in mind that your experience is bound to be different from mine.

Some of my advice may not always help. And you'll learn plenty of other stuff that I haven't covered at all.

Whatever happens, though, I hope you hang on to one thing, which is what I said at the very start: that you can have a happy, prosperous freelance career without having to change your essential character as an introvert.

I've tried to open the door and show you the way. What happens next is up to you. Good luck!

> ### Please review!
>
> If you enjoyed this book, please take five minutes to write a positive review on Amazon.
>
> It would mean a lot to me, and it will help more freelance introverts like you discover the book.
>
> Thank you!

About the author

Tom Albrighton has been a freelance copywriter for over 12 years.

In that time, he's written about everything from cupcakes and cameras to spectacles and solar panels, working for household names like Prudential, Jeyes and Fuji, as well as dozens of small businesses and marketing agencies.

Tom is also a co-founder of ProCopywriters, the UK alliance of commercial writers. In a 2015 DMA survey, he was ranked the #7 'Copywriter rated by copywriters'.

By the same author:

Copywriting Made Simple

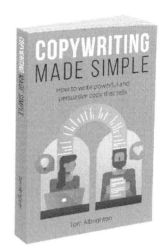

Copywriting is writing with purpose.

It's about using words to reach people and change what they think, feel and do.

This easy-to-read guide will teach you all the essentials of copywriting, from understanding products, readers and benefits to closing the sale.

It's packed with real-life examples that will show you exactly how the ideas and techniques will work in the real world.

And with dozens of useful illustrations and diagrams, *Copywriting Made Simple* shows you the ideas that other books just talk about.

Plus there's a whole chapter of handy tips on writing ads, websites, broadcast media, direct mail, social media and print.

Copywriting Made Simple is the perfect introduction to copywriting today.

Find it on Amazon or learn more at **copywritingmadesimple.info**.

By the same author:

Cash Money Freelancing

So, you've gone freelance. And you're making a living. But have you made yourself a life?

Freelancing should set you free. But for some, it's more like a prison sentence – because they just don't make enough money.

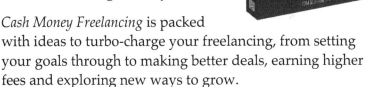

Cash Money Freelancing is packed with ideas to turbo-charge your freelancing, from setting your goals through to making better deals, earning higher fees and exploring new ways to grow.

Here's what you'll learn…

- Why you need a 'money mind' as well as a 'work mind'
- How to understand the unique value you offer
- The best ways to charge – and what to charge for
- How to present your prices more persuasively
- How to negotiate price deals like a pro
- Proven techniques for increasing your rates
- How to be less like a sole trader and more like a business.

If you've got the skills, the work and the clients, but your freelance business still isn't jumping the way it should, *Cash Money Freelancing* has the answers you need.

Find it on Amazon in paperback and ebook.

Printed in Great Britain
by Amazon